THE FOOL AND THE MAGICIAN

A MEMOIR OF LOVE TOLD IN TAROT READINGS

ANGELA LAM

CONTENTS

ADVANCE PRAISE

Lam's memoir uniquely blends an exploration of love, relationships, mental health, with the more mystical and magical original elements. Her vulnerability and nuanced emotional states allow readers to truly connect to her profound and intimate story.

—Publishers Weekly The BookLife Prize

Publishing History
First Edition, 2022
Print ISBN 979-8-9857935-0-5
Digital ISBN 979-8-9857935-1-2

For Ed

AUTHOR'S NOTE

This is a work of creative nonfiction. In it, I describe experiences that had a profound effect on me and those I love. The events in this book are true to the best of my knowledge and recollection. In writing this memoir, I relied upon my personal journals, date and time stamped photographs, court documents, text messages, emails, letters, books, and interviews. For readability, I altered the order of a few of the events or I changed the sequence of the tarot cards. Since I was intoxicated for a good portion of the dissolution of my marriage, I do not pretend that I am capable of remembering everything that took place exactly or offering every person's perspective, especially those closest to the matter. To add cultural and historical perspective, I interviewed tarot readers and women who used tarot to help them make major life decisions. I also read several books on the history of tarot and took an online course to further develop my tarot reading skills. To protect the privacy of real individuals, I have changed some names or modified some identifying details.

"What is wrong cannot be made right,
What is missing cannot be recovered."
—Ecclesiastes 1:15

INTRODUCTION

I originally structured my midlife memoir into
tarot readings as a literary device without any
thought of further implications. I just drew the
cards and picked the scenes from my life that
corresponded with the meaning. I used the Rider-
Waite -Smith tarot deck, the most popular tarot
deck in the world. First published in 1909, the
Rider-Waite-Smith tarot deck was written by
Arthur Waite, a Christian mystic, illustrated by
Paula Colman Smith, and published by William
Rider and Sons of London. The deck experienced
resurgence in popularity when U.S. Games
Systems, Inc. republished it in 1971.

I was born in 1971 to a mother whose birthday
fell on April Fools' Day.

Daughter of the Fool, I became one, too. I
trusted faith more than reason and seldom looked
before I leaped.

That's why I discovered the need to include a
cultural and historical perspective on the tarot

after I completed this manuscript. Of particular interest was why women seek answers from tarot readings. After talking with several tarot card readers and women who practice the tarot, I discovered women primarily turn to the tarot for guidance and direction. Often these women are overwhelmed with responsibilities and have lost touch with their intuition. Tarot reading becomes a source of empowerment, a tool for introspection and healing.

My belief and practice in tarot is slightly different. Whenever I am stuck and feel I have not received any response from God or any peace through meditation, I pick up the cards to glimpse into the future. I need reassurance that everything will turn out all right or, if not, then I will at least be alerted to any pitfalls in the journey ahead. Awareness is everything, right? You can't solve a problem you aren't aware of, and tarot can illuminate many potholes. In my experience, Major Arcana cards not only represent big events such as birth, death, marriage, and divorce, they signal things outside of my control—fate, destiny, and the future. Minor Arcana cards, on the other hand, deal with things completely within my grasp—the daily choices I make that influence the final outcome. When I see both cards in my spread, I focus on the interplay of the things outside of my control (Major Arcana) and the things within my control (Minor Arcana) to determine how I get to the stated, or most likely, outcome.

Paul Quinn, author of *Tarot for Life*, wrote that someone who asks questions about the future acknowledges a genuine powerlessness to influ-

ence events. I disagree. Like tarot reader Sinead
Fine and women's spirituality and tarot expert
Rachel Pollack, I believe we have free will regardless of how we use the tarot. However, according
to Pollack, the freedom of choice is rare because
we seldom bring ourselves to the level of
consciousness needed to act outside the parame-
ters of history, psychological wounds, social
conditioning, or even the habit of routine. This
perspective of free choice transcends my level of
understanding and experience, but I have started
to consider this point of view as not only valid but
essential to a deeper understanding of the tarot
and human nature.

This memoir, therefore, is a compilation of my
personal experience interspersed with threads of
how tarot influenced the choices I made in my life,
particularly in regards to marriage. This is my
journey. Yours may be different. If I have learned
anything from my research, it is this—the tarot is
highly individualistic.

GLOSSARY

Empress: a Major Arcana card representing fertility, femininity, and motherhood or a woman who displays these characteristics.

Fool: a Major Arcana card representing someone who takes a leap of faith; the character in the hero's journey who travels from unconsciousness to consciousness; new beginnings.

Knight of Cups: a Minor Arcana card representing a romantic man in a love reading; or in a career reading, a job offer or opportunity.

Magician: a Major Arcana card representing mastery over one's talents; tapping into one's full potential.

Major Arcana: the 22 cards in a tarot deck that depict mythological, allegorical, archetypal, astrological, and spiritual images such as the Moon, the

Tower, the Hanged Man, and the High Priestess. Typically, these cards contain a lot of universal energy and appear when one is going through a major growth period. In my personal experience, these cards reflect things outside of one's control, such as the environment, the choices of others, and destiny.

Minor Arcana: the remaining 56 cards in a tarot deck. These cards are divided into four suits: wands, cups, pentacles, and swords. These four suits reflect the suits of a standard playing deck of cards. Wands represent creativity, from the spark of inspiration to the manifestation of a completed project. Cups reflect the emotional aspects of our lives. Pentacles are anything grounded in the physicality of the world, from economics to our bodies to the earth. Swords represent mental challenges we face and the words we use to communicate to one another. The cards are numbered ace through ten and include a set of court cards—pages, knights, queens, and kings. Some tarot readers interpret the court cards as actual people. In my experience, the court cards can also represent the opportunities brought to one through individuals or reflect the level of maturity in our lives. A page is someone who is young or childish. A knight is someone who is more on the cusp of adolescence and adulthood. A queen and king are adults who reflect the most mature aspects of feminine or masculine energy.

Page of Swords: an intelligent young man full of energy, passion, and enthusiasm but who is immature.

Querent: the person who asks for a reading, usually with a specific question in mind.

Reader: someone who has studied tarot cards and knows how to answer the Querent's question.

Reading: interpretation of a tarot spread.

Spread: an arrangement of tarot cards used to answer the Querent's question. Several spreads exist, from the one card spread for simple yes or no questions to the more complicated spreads such as the Celtic Cross, a placement of ten cards with each card referencing a specific aspect of the Querent's question.

Tarot: a deck of 78 illustrated cards divided between Major Arcana and Minor Arcana used for various purposes, such as entertainment, divination, fortune-telling, introspection, guidance, intuition, healing, and wellness. The first tarot deck was patterned after standard playing cards in the 1400's. In 1909, William Rider and Sons of London published the Rider-Waite Deck written by Arthur Waite and illustrated by Pamela Colman Smith. U.S. Games Systems, Inc. republished the cards as the Rider Tarot Deck in 1971. Today, the Rider-Waite-Smith tarot deck is the most popular tarot deck in the world. Hundreds of thousands of other tarot decks exist and can be readily purchased online or at retailers.

TAROT READING 1

WILL WE GET MARRIED?

Yes/No One Card Tarot Reading

*J*uly 1991: The World
    I am sitting cross-legged on the day bed in the living room of our two-bedroom apartment, crying into the phone.

"Calm down," Laura says. "I can't understand what you're saying."

One month ago, I moved 110 miles north from San Jose to Santa Rosa, California, to start a new life with you. But I am unhappy. I aborted a child I wanted to give up for adoption, and I am surprised by the level of grief I experienced.

When my blubbering descends into senseless sobbing, she asks, "Do you need me to drive up and give you a reading?"

Whenever a crisis strikes, Laura turns to tarot readings. As a Unitarian, she believes tarot cards reflect multiple spiritual beliefs, from Egyptian Rosicrucianism, Anglo-Saxon paganism, Christian Hermeticism, and Jewish mysticism. As the daughter of a Jungian sociology professor and a hippie artist-turned-elementary school teacher, she practices tarot readings to access the deepest part of herself, the self she cannot reach through a combination of prayer, meditation, and psychotherapy.

Laura is not the only one who relies on tarot readings. According to Sinead Fine, a tarot reader located in Israel, women from around the world contact her for a tarot reading whenever they are overwhelmed and confused. Most women ask about relationships followed by health. Men, on the other hand, mostly consult her about their careers followed by relationships. According to Fine, both men and women seem out of touch with their intuition, unable to access the wisdom stored in their bodies and minds. Tarot readings, therefore, offer clarity and guidance.

The next weekend, Laura travels two hours to see me, bringing her tarot deck wrapped in a black velvet pouch. We sit cross-legged on the shag carpet of the living room. I shuffle the cards and close my eyes and think of my question. When I open my eyes, I watch Laura turn over a card: The World. Typically, this card signifies the end of one period of life and the beginning of a new one. But when I see the image of a person dancing on top of the world, I think, If I get married to you, the whole world will be mine. Every time we have sex I fear another unwanted pregnancy even though we are using two forms of birth control now. When I see a pregnant woman in the grocery store, in church, or walking down the street, I burst into tears. That could have been me, I think. Even your words haunt me when you comfort and console me. You say, "It would be different if we were married." I start to equate marriage with an insurance policy against a second unwanted pregnancy and abortion.

Staring at the card, I don't say what I feel. I only clutch a fist to my chest and cry.

Laura pats my shoulder and reassures me. "Don't worry. The cards never lie."

∾

SEPTEMBER 1991

I WAKE IN THE MIDDLE OF THE NIGHT TO SOMEONE pawing my arms. Scrunching my face, I bat my hands, searching for the culprit in the dark.

You, my Magician, fumble beneath the sheets.

"What are you doing?" I blink and squint in the shadows.

Ignoring the nettles in my voice, you grasp my cold hand in your warm fingers. "Will you marry me?"

The bite of metal knocks against my knuckle and spins at the base of the third finger of my left hand. "It's too big," I say, struggling to sit.

"Will you marry me?" you ask again. You curl my fingers into a fist so the too-big-ring does not slide off into the bed.

"Yes, of course." I have been begging you for months to propose to me. "But put this away so I won't lose it." I tuck the ring into your palm. "I need to take it to a jeweler to be sized."

In the morning, when I wake in the watery light of our two bedroom apartment, I find the white box on the dresser and flip open the lid. The solitaire winks at me. I cover my mouth with both hands and gasp. Prickles of delight travel from the bottom of my feet to the crown of my head. I squeal, "You bought the big one!" Two weekends ago, we window shopped at the mall, and you asked me to try on rings "just for fun." I thought I was a fool, choosing the larger of the two tiny diamond rings in the display case, a perfect solitaire in yellow gold. The sales clerk, asking about our budget, suggested the smaller, imperfect stone. I cringed, taking off the ring with disgust. "That black dot looks exactly like the wart on the bottom of my left foot that the doctor just froze off."

But you didn't buy the black-dot-diamond. You bought the perfect stone, which costs more than six months of your income.

No one has spent that much money on me.

You swagger out of the shower, a towel cinched around your waist, and snicker. "I wanted to put the ring on my penis to propose to you. But the opening is too small." You drop your towel and whirl your penis around like a Ferris wheel.

What would you do with a ring on a penis?

4

Plop it into my mouth? I snap the box shut. "Why couldn't you propose like a normal man?"

"Am I normal?" You cock an eyebrow and wave a hand along the chiseled muscles of your sides.

Sighing, I shake my head. Of course, you aren't. You're the Magician, the master of illusion, the second card in the tarot deck. You are unconventional, full of surprises. Every reason why I love you reinforces how I am the Fool, the first card in the tarot deck, full of faith and folly. We are Major Arcana cards, meaning we are part of each other's destiny. Nothing can stop us from being together. Only God or fate can tear us apart.

But right now I want us to be only a man and a woman.

I throw my arms wide. "What am I supposed to say when people ask how you proposed?"

Shrugging, you tug a shirt over your head and step into your boxer briefs. "Tell them the truth."

"That you woke me up in the middle of the night to slip a too-big-ring on my finger?" Annoyed, I pace across the worn carpet and thread my fingers through my tangled hair. "You didn't even get down on one knee. And you wanted to stick your dick in my mouth." I shudder.

"I got down on one knee." You step into your shoes, the shoes you don't bother to tie, the laces permanently knotted.

I glower at your feet. Will our children learn to wear their shoes like you, assuming we have children other than the one we aborted?

You grab the box, kneel, and withdraw the ring. Holding it up like a communion wafer, you ask once again, "Will you marry me?"

I twist my lips into a frown then a smile. Emotion wells up in my eyes. You aren't the most romantic man, but you're my man. "Yes," I whisper.

The tarot card was right.

One part of my life—being single—has ended.

The next part of my life—being married—has begun.

TAROT READING 2

⚜

CAN THIS MARRIAGE BE SAVED?

A Ten Card Celtic Cross Tarot Reading

*A*pril 2010: I have been married to you, my Magician, since August 1992. We have two children: a fifteen-year-old son who has autism, cerebral palsy, and global developmental delay who we call our Forever Child and a ten-year-old neurotypical daughter who we refer to as our Princess Pea. This morning while washing the cars, I discover a greeting card tucked between the passenger's seat and the center

7

console of the your SUV. I consult with Melanie, a tarot reader, who predicts our future in a ten card Celtic Cross reading. The first card represents my interpretation of the present situation. I pick the Ten of Swords, which typically means the end of a long, mentally-challenging battle. Tens are the final cards in the Minor Arcana and represent the culmination of that suit. Swords are associated with masculinity, intellect, sorrow, and misfortune. In the Rider-Waite-Smith tarot, the picture on the card shows a man lying face down with ten swords protruding from his back. In the distance, behind the mountains, the sun has begun to rise. With the end of strife come surrender and the promise of a new day. But first, the Querent must deal with the hurt, fear, overwhelm, and doubt of the situation. There is no space or time or ability to run away.

~

A JOLT OF FEAR POWERS THROUGH MY BODY, ticking off the internal alarm system—thick cords braid up the backs of my legs, a cold stone plunks to the bottom of my stomach, and a swarm of bees unleashes in my chest. I storm into the house and thrust the card beneath your nose while you are typing on your laptop and watching TV. "Who gave *this* to you?"

You crane back your neck, peer at the card through your reading glasses, and raise an eyebrow. "No one. It was a surprise for you."

The tectonic plates rearrange on your face. I duck and cover, bracing against the next sentence.

"Why do you always have to ruin my surprises?"

I steady my legs. The breath catches in my throat. I gasp, choke, heave, and suck in air. *I* ruin your surprises? I jab a finger at the inside of the card. "This isn't your handwriting."

You shrug, turn back to your computer screen, and resume typing. "I'm sorry you don't recognize my handwriting. I wrote the note without my glasses. I wanted to surprise you."

Surprise me, you did, my Magician. From out of nothing comes tangible evidence of what I've suspected for the past two years—an affair with one of your clients.

My heartbeat thumps against my ribs like fists pounding against a cage, ready to burst free, to flee this sham of a marriage. Every night I come home and take care of our children while you are somewhere out there with another woman, pretending to indulge in the fantasy world depicted on the front of the greeting card, a trop-ical paradise of sand and sunshine, hugs and kisses, each moment an escape from the past twenty-four hours.

Our daughter shuffles through the living room and into the kitchen, peering at the stove. "Where's the coffee cake?" She has your brown hair, my almond-shaped eyes, your chipmunk cheeks dotted with freckles, and a body as sturdy as the Lego buildings she constructs in her bedroom after she's finished her homework.

Every Saturday morning for the past ten years, after I wash and detail both cars, I bake homemade coffee cake from the Betty Crocker recipe book my mother bought as a wedding gift. I serve it warm with a cup of juice as breakfast for the children. I force a smile. "I haven't made it yet."

"May I help you, Mama?"

"Sure." I can use some assistance. "Let me finish cleaning the insides of the cars. I'll come get you when I'm ready, okay?"

Our daughter nods, rubs her eyes, and disappears down the hallway.

I drop the card and envelope into your lap. The bits of evidence float to your keyboard.

You seize the card and the envelope and tuck them beside your hip and the recliner.

I leave the house. The bees have flown from the hive. The stone has dissolved from the pit of the stomach. The knots have unraveled from the backs of the thighs. The sun breaks through the gray, overcast sky and shines hot against my face. I'll never see the card or the envelope again, but I'll remember they exist. If the card was meant for me, you would have opened the front door as soon as you woke up and padded out in your T-shirt and shorts and bare feet and asked, "Did you find the surprise I left for you on the kitchen table?" You would have waited, suspended like the Hang Man at a crossroads. Only after I acknowledged the token of love and appreciation with a flick of my gaze or the hint of a smile would you have wrapped your arms around me, pulled me close, and kissed me until I grew dizzy and limp in your embrace. You would have gazed at me with your sky blue eyes, as vast and hopeful as any spring day, and said, "I love you and no one else."

$\backsim$

THE SECOND CARD IN THE CELTIC CROSS READING represents the past events influencing the present situation. I draw Justice, a Major Arcana card. Major Arcana cards represent karmic lessons, archetypal struggles, and cosmic forces beyond one's control. In the Rider-Waite-Smith tarot, crowned and robed, Justice sits on a throne with a raised sword in one hand and a scale balanced in the other hand. Karma, the laws of cause and effect, and truth are all represented in this card. Justice in the past means the events of today are fair and just when compared to what has previously transpired.

∼

I MAY BE THE FOOL, BUT I AM NOT INNOCENT.

I have cheated long before you, my Magician.

Depending on the interpretation, these incidences may be justified, vilified, or nullified.

Here is the list (some of these you know about; others you don't, or maybe you do, and I am ignorant):

1. Will, otherwise known as "the guy from the gym." He stole my mind before he stole a kiss.
2. James, the on-again, off-again lover who coached me in writing. You remind me I probably wouldn't have been with him if I had not injured my back in a warehouse accident. True, you wouldn't have had to work two jobs while I healed and retrained. But I think the real reason why I bonded with him was over

the loss of our first child who I aborted, the one I couldn't help but think was normal, not like our Forever Child with his multiple disabilities. Grief, that harbinger of all things destructive, drove me into his arms. When I finally withdrew all of my individual money from savings, packed my bags, and towed our three-year-old son to his apartment to be his full-time girlfriend, he returned me to you on the same day. I didn't know I was refundable like a wrong-sized T-shirt. You graciously welcomed me home like the prodigal son. To this day, I don't know why. Yes, you say the reason was love, but even I know love is never enough. I'll never understand your devotion and loyalty under those extenuating circumstances.

3. Wanna Be Don Juan – you suspected the affair but the relationship evolved into something else, and since I promised to never reveal the guy's identity, I will keep that promise.

4. Anthony, the jeweler masquerading as an attorney. My intention was to experience a one-night stand, not a six-month nightmare. Between his penchant for lies and insatiable lust and my need for fantasy and never-ending escape, we elongated the meet-cute in front of a downtown coffee shop to a lobster salad lunch at the marina to a blow job at his studio apartment on the

air mattress he purchased after his wife took the memory foam queen-size mattress to her mother's house three cities away while waiting for the divorce to become final. He wore a condom (didn't want to get tested first) and I gummed him until he came, all the while being careful to not further injure the tooth I knocked loose from eating the steak you cooked for me on Valentine's Day. Afterward, we walked side by side down the residential street. I stopped on the bridge above the trickling summer creek, leaning on my elbows, letting the guilt soak through my business suit like sweat. "You're angry with yourself, not me," Anthony said. As an experienced adulterer, he spoke the one truth between us. I didn't want to lose our marriage like he had lost his, so when he invited me over for a threesome during my lunch break, I declined. A handful of months later, he called, asking for one more chance. After all, he was dying of skin cancer from too many afternoons lounging without sun screen on the deck of his friend's yacht. Just a quickie for old times? The answer was no.

You may suspect there were others. Of course, my imagination often traveled there just as yours did.

Let's be fair and list our offenses:

You—pornography, online dating sites, and yearly trips to Las Vegas strip clubs.

Me—the carousel of you-me-him, the creation of fake online profiles in the hopes of "catching" you in the act of flirtation, and an obsession with the differences between love and sex.

Let's agree the discovery of the greeting card wedged between the center console and the passenger's seat of your SUV left me with no right to be angry. After all, I've done worse to you.

∼

THE THIRD CARD IN THE CELTIC CROSS READING represents the message from one's higher self, the consciousness that mingles with the eternal, the part of us that is all knowing, all seeing, all believing, that seeks the highest good, forever concerned with the inter-connected well-being of all things. I select the Death card, which in the context of my question, "Can this marriage be saved?" typically means the dynamics of the relationship are keeping both parties stuck, and if the relationship is to survive, both parties must release the past to move forward or face an unexpected and unwanted change. In the Rider-Waite-Smith deck, the image on the card shows a skeleton in armor riding a white horse across a battlefield where bodies lie and children kneel and a bishop offers worship. In the distance, the sun shines between two white pillars. The image echoes the Tree of Life and the ascension of Jesus three days after his death and resurrection. The Querent who draws this card is asked to awaken into consciousness, to become fully alive, releasing old, unneeded habits. Rarely does Death indicate a physical dying. Most of the time this card symbolizes change, generation, evolution, and letting go to make room for the new.

～

FIFTY DOLLARS. THAT'S ALL THE MONEY I HAVE LEFT. I scrounge around the bottom of my purse, searching for loose change and double check the inside zippered pocket in the event I stashed a couple of extra dollars when I was too much in a hurry to place the bills in my wallet. *Nothing.*

I can't sit here much longer. Without air conditioning, the inside of my twelve-year-old four-door sedan is an inferno. The heat plasters my bangs to my forehead and sweat streams in rivulets down my sides.

Fifty dollars will either fill my tank for a month or buy groceries for a few days or pay for a half hour tarot reading.

I start the engine and back out of the parking space in the glass and steel business park where I work part-time for a private money lender whose business has dried up with the Great Recession. Although I do not want to leave the mom-and-pop enterprise, I am following the advice of the family law attorney I recently consulted—marriage counseling and a full-time job with health benefits.

The counseling has been arranged through my current therapist who referred me to her friend in the same adobe office building on the corner of College and Beaver streets.

The job search has led me on a wild goose

chase from San Francisco to Ukiah without any offers.

From what you told me last night, we have only one month's income saved before we end up in the 90 day foreclosure process, possibly losing our home. After devoting ten years of saving for the down payment, I do not want our investment to be another casualty in the financial crisis. Even if one of us must surrender fifty percent to the other in a divorce, at least the children will have some place to call home.

After a short drive, I pull into the parking lot of Crystal Channels to meet with Melanie, a tarot card reader. During my teens and twenties, whenever I faced an apparently insurmountable situation, Laura, my best friend at the time, would remove a set of tarot cards encased in a black velvet pouch and tell me to shuffle, silently asking my question and placing my energy into the deck. Through tarot readings, I decided to leave my first serious boyfriend to date you. Since then, whenever therapy, prayer, and logic fail to relieve stuck feelings, I turn to the tarot to unleash hidden wisdom. According to a 2009 study by Pew Research Center, roughly six-in-ten Americans engage in multiple religious practices, mixing elements of diverse traditions, including Christianity and the occult. By 2018, six-in-ten Americans regardless of their religious beliefs will hold at least one New Age belief such as reincarnation or astrology. By 2019, *The New York Times* will have an article about how alternative practices, such as tarot, factor into traditional psychotherapy. In 2021, *The National Catholic Reporter* will have an article centered on findings from Springtide Research Institute showing fifty-one percent of people between the ages of thirteen and twenty-five combining their traditional religious beliefs with the practice of tarot reading because of the widespread influence of the internet and social media.

But this is the summer of 2010, and I am a thirty-nine-year-old Catholic woman seeking answers from God. I cannot find any reliable statistics about how many people believe in the divinatory powers of tarot. All I know is I want a glimpse into the future to discover if I find a job in time to save our house from foreclosure. Knowing what will happen is comforting. I can prepare for better or for worse. I do not have to go by faith alone into the unknown. I can walk confidently, armed for whatever the future will bring.

I met Melanie a few years ago while searching for crystals to heal the shattered despondency I felt after losing James. I don't remember what cards were drawn or what was spoken between us. I only remember the cloud of despair lifting from my spirit. Since then, I've respected Melanie's talents. I am confident my appointment with her today will enlighten my fruitless job search.

The tiny bell on the glass door announces my arrival. A chill from the air conditioning shimmies up my back. Seconds later, Melanie steps out of a curtained alcove smelling of sandalwood and amber incense. She reminds me of an older version of Laura's mother, a former hippie artist-turned-elementary school teacher. Long white hair frames her cherubic face. A colorful caftan conceals her shapeless body. Leather sandals cover her broad feet. She smiles sweetly when she shakes my sweaty hand.

After taking a seat at the small round table, I clutch my purse in my lap and breathe in deeply.

Melanie releases the curtain, shielding us from the foot traffic in the two room store, and sets out her garden tarot deck on the table. "What's bothering you today?"

I exhale loudly, my shoulders slumping forward. "I've been searching for a new job the last few weeks, but I haven't found anything."

Nodding, she shuffles the cards and deals them into a circle. Turning the first card over, she touches the petals of a sunflower. "You're looking for a job that will use your skills, something you'll excel in, a job in which you will go far, much farther than you've been able to before." She meets my gaze and smiles. "Aren't we all looking for a job like that?"

I nod in agreement. *So far, so good.*

She turns over the next card. "You've taken jobs to get by, and you're not opposed to doing that again."

Fiddling with the straps of my purse, I recall all of the jobs I've applied for over the past 30 days, including jobs in which I am qualified for but do not want. I sigh. Even the last interview at a sandwich shop didn't pan out when the owner took one look at my business suit and said, "You're too good to scrub toilets." I protested, claiming, "I clean my bathrooms at home." But he shook his head and escorted me to my car, unconvinced.

Flipping over the next card, she strokes the

petals of a pink daisy and frowns. "Two jobs are competing for your attention—one is close to home; the other is far away. You'll do well in either position."

I lean closer, clutching the purse straps tighter. I have applied for a loan servicing position at an attorney-operated private money enterprise in San Rafael, a forty-five minute drive away, and a loan documentation administrator position at a community bank, five minutes from my house.

She reveals the next card. "You'll take the job close to home."

I smile, and relief washes over me.

After turning over the final card, she hitches her breath. "When you're there, you'll meet a man who will heal your heart."

Frowning, I lean forward. "What do you mean? I'm looking for a job, not a boyfriend."

She sits back and chuckles. "My dear, this man is not a boyfriend."

I glower at the card of a metal armet and pink eglantine flowers winding around golden chalices. "I'm not looking for a one-night stand or a part-time lover." After Anthony, I vowed to never befriend any man as a potential romantic interest.

She touches my hand. "My dear, this man is not a one-night stand or a part-time lover." She leans closer and squeezes my cold fingers. "This man is your next husband."

I gasp, and my purse rolls off my lap and hits the floor. The contents scatter—keys, wallet, phone, lipstick, panty liner, tissues, checkbook, and eyeglass cases. Kneeling, I gather my belongings and struggle to suck oxygen from the suddenly too thin air. *Husband?* "But I'm already married. We're going to couples' counseling. We're working things out." I choke, handing her the last money I have until my next paltry paycheck. "We're happy."

She slides the fifty dollars beneath the deck of cards and nods. "Of course, you are, my dear. That's why you're looking for a better job. That's why you're attending marriage counseling." She points to the bills tucked beneath the cards. "That's why you just gave me all the money you have."

I snap to attention, zipping up my purse, and shoving the strap over my shoulder. I didn't tell her anything about how much money I have. "I don't want a second husband. I'm Catholic. Marriage is for *life*." I spit out the last word like a death sentence.

She nods and folds her hands across her waist. "I am not challenging your beliefs. I only read the cards, and the cards never lie. Neither one of us can change destiny."

"A second husband is not destiny." I pull back the curtain and step into the incense-filled store. Regret pummels through me. I just wasted fifty dollars. How could I be so foolish? I stalk out of the air conditioned store, the bells tinkling behind me, and duck into the blazing inferno of my four-door sedan and speed home.

∾

The fourth card in the Celtic Cross reading represents the preoccupation of one's subconscious.

These thoughts, feelings, and impulses may be hidden, but they greatly influence one's behavior. When the subconscious is out of tune with the conscious, rational mind, chaos can ensue. I have drawn another Major Arcana card, the Moon, which typically means emotions are complicated during this time. Pamela Colman Smith listened to Beethoven's Symphony No. 5 when she illustrated this card which showcases a moon shining between two white towers, which appears eerily identical to the sun shining between two white towers in the Death card. A dog and a wolf howl at the moon, and a crawfish rises from the waters. Arthur Waite said the wild and tame animals reflect the mind's movement from the known to the unknown, which Swiss psychologist Carl Jung later referred to as one's shadow, the part of the personality one doesn't want to acknowledge. On a mundane note, the moon with its cyclical nature mirrors the female menstrual cycle. If culture has anything to do with this reading, the Chinese believe the moon represents lunacy. Craziness, whether from one's shadow or hormonal shifts, disturbs all relationships. One should look deeper and explore the undercurrents of the situation before making any decisions because everything on the surface may not be what it appears to be. Trust one's intuition. Examine one's dreams. Believe in premonitions.

∼

AFTER THE CHILDREN ARE IN BED AND YOU'VE EATEN dinner and settled in the living room to read the news on your laptop, I wander into the room to tell you about Melanie's prediction about the job and the second husband.

You look up from your laptop and ask, "This isn't God talking to you, is it?"

"No, I had a tarot reading." Frowning, I place a hand on my hip. "God didn't talk to me."

You relax against the back of the recliner and resume reading the news online.

"Just because God didn't talk to me doesn't mean this prediction isn't real." I sit on the ottoman by your extraordinarily large feet for your average body, the same feet your grandfather used to tease you about as a child by saying, "Don't know about the building, but the foundation's good."

I clasp my hands between my knees, bow my head, and sigh. How can I communicate with you in a way you'll understand? Although God does talk to me (not all the time, only when necessary, which means once every few years), I also believe we can communicate with God in other ways (prayer, meditation, nature, and tarot readings, being a few of them).

"I'm not just Catholic," I say. "I come from a long line of Chinese mystics." According to author Muriel Barbery, Asian cultures accept and honor the mystery of being here, in this life and in this world, better than cultures in the West that require a logical explanation.

"Yeah, I know." You keep your gaze focused on the laptop screen. "Your whole family is crazy."

"We're not crazy." I slap my hands on my thighs and bristle with irritation.

You scoff. "Every time I see your family, I hear another tall tale." You shake your head and huff. "Your dad is full of stories. Like the time he fell off a cable car when he was younger and his soul visited heaven, but he was sent back to earth because they weren't ready for him. Or the time your dad was visited by his father's ghost before the ship's captain told him he was going on family leave because his dad just died."

"Extraordinary things don't just happen to my dad." I straighten my spine. "Have I ever told you about my aunt Lil?"

You close your laptop. "What about her?"

"My father's only sister fell in love with a man Mah-Mah refused to let her marry because he came from a different Chinese community. Aunt Lil was distraught. She wouldn't eat or sleep. My dad thought she would die of grief. But one day, a blue dragonfly visited Mah-Mah and told her to let Aunt Lil marry the man. My dad insists that blue dragonfly was his father who came back from the dead to reassure Mah-Mah that Aunt Lil's boyfriend would be good to her. Mah-Mah allowed the marriage, and they've been happily married ever since."

You stare at me with your unblinking blue eyes. You don't look convinced.

I stand and pace. "My father can predict the future."

"How?"

I glance around the living room where we've been sitting this past half hour while the children are asleep. I cross my arms over my chest and huddle near you. I've never told this story to anyone. But how else will you believe me?

"When I was at Northwestern University, my father sent me an article about date rape. During our weekly phone calls, he warned me about a boy I had not met yet. He reminded me to use the self-defense he had taught me when I was younger. I thought he was crazy. Three weeks later, I met a musician. We went to get gelato and walk along Lake Michigan. The guy pinned me to the pier and shoved his tongue in my mouth and grappled with my shirt. I remembered what my father said. I twisted the boy's pinkie until the joint almost broke, and he immediately released me." I slump on the ottoman and sigh. Closing my eyes, I rub a hand across my sweaty forehead. I don't care anymore whether or not you believe in premonitions, in fate, in destiny, in witnessing the future. I'm tired. I want to go to bed.

You reach around the laptop and pat my shoulder. "Don't worry about the tarot reader's prediction. You haven't even been offered a job. How can this stranger come between us?"

I open my eyes and meet your calm gaze. You seem so confident, so sure. That magical ability you have of transforming all of my worries into dust works. I kiss you and tell you I'm heading to bed. You tell me you will join me shortly.

As I brush my teeth, I think how silly I've been to place all of my trust in a tarot card reading.

Without a credible threat from a visible stranger, we have no enemy to battle. Why talk about strategy over something we cannot see?

I lie in bed, waiting for you to join me. I am wearing one of the pieces of lingerie your friend from high school sells on her online adult sensuality shop. You helped her build and optimize the website, and she paid you with merchandise. Out of all of the erotic pieces, this particular item I like best—a periwinkle blue and silver peek-a-boo gown. The frilly lace tickles my skin and the filmy material fails to keep me warm. From where I lie on our bed, I can gaze out the door and down the hall at the light from the living room. Your fingers tap dance on the keyboard, keeping time like a percussion instrument.

When you are finished working, you will close your laptop, turn off the living room light, pad into our bedroom and close the door. You will brush your teeth, strip naked, and hold me tight. As we tangle up in each other's arms, neither one of us will mention the tarot card reading. Its presence will sink to the bottom of our collective consciousness like a pebble, seemingly small and insignificant, until it is completely out of sight.

∼

THE NEXT CARD IN THE CELTIC CROSS READING represents the positive forces that will help answer the question, "Can this marriage be saved?" I draw the Six of Cups. An image of two children exchanging a cup full of flowers greets me. Smiling, I am reminded of the days when we were first married and you saved part of your lunch money during the week to buy me a bouquet of flowers from the corner florist during your Friday commute home. The memory triggers the warmth of nostalgia—kind, loving feelings from past events.

Arthur Waite wrote of this card, "Things that have vanished." In this light, the tenderness I feel is for things that are no longer part of our lives. Sadly, I don't remember the last time you bought me flowers.

*I think of my high school English teacher who had
been married twice. He always said whenever he and
his current wife fought he focused on how trivial the
matter at hand was in comparison to the history
between them. You and I have been together all of our
adult lives, but we met earlier. I find comfort in the
fond memories between us.*

∼

YOU WERE SEVENTEEN GOING ON EIGHTEEN AND I
was sixteen going on seventeen when we first met.
Although we didn't attend the same high school (I
was at the new campus originally designed to be a
junior college, complete with an Olympic-sized
pool while you attended my mother's alma mater),
we had a friend in common—the Page of Swords,
an intelligent, young man who attended the local
junior college and who tutored me in economics.
He liked reading *The Hitchhiker's Guide to the
Galaxy* and *Brave New World* and cruising up and
down Highway 101 in Northern California,
hiking the Santa Cruz Mountains, and hanging
out at Craig's parents' house in the hot tub
beneath a canopy of stars and views of Silicon
Valley.

The summer before my senior year of high
school, just weeks before I left for Northwestern
University as a Cherub scholar, I sat a round table
with the Page of Swords and his friends eating
lunch at Sizzler.

You arrived late, and at first I thought you had
the wrong table, but you stood beside the Page of
Swords and bowed your head and conversed. I

remember thinking, *That guy is too good-looking to be the Page of Swords' friend.* I was used to hanging out with a bunch of tall, burly, overweight college-aged men in glasses, baggy shirts, and khaki pants. You, on the other hand, were short and fit from being on the track and cross country and wrestling teams. You wore your brown hair in a part down the middle and feathered on both sides like Shaun Cassidy from the seventies. You also sported a tiny mustache like a dash above your lips. The turquoise blue Polo shirt matched the color of your eyes, and the slim faded jeans hugged your well-developed thighs. A shock of energy pulverized my solar plexus, and I thought, *I really like this guy,* without having a reason. After all, you were a stranger. I didn't know anything about you. That's how powerful your magic was. Years later, I would realize we had a lot in common, from our bittersweet childhoods to our overwhelming ambitions.

In spite of the initial attraction on my end, you avoided me. You had a knack of disappearing no matter what social event we attended together. You dodged me at the San Jose Civic Center after we walked along the Youth Hall of Fame and I pointed out the plaque with my name on it as the youngest byline reporter for the San Jose Mercury News. At parties, you always massaged the shoulders of the females in attendance, except for me. Whenever I asked for a massage, you said, "You're next," but when my turn came, you suddenly had to leave.

Over time, I became the girlfriend to the Page of Swords since I needed a date to my senior ball and all of the guys I had asked who attended my high school had declined the invitation. The Page of Swords agreed to be my date, and that opened the door to the first serious relationship I had.

Although older and wiser, the Page of Swords wasn't an ideal boyfriend. He prioritized friendship over romance. The majority of our dates consisted of attending parties where I saw you, his best friend, amidst a house full of teens and young adults drinking sodas and eating pizza. We geeks and nerds didn't smoke pot or drink alcohol. We wanted to keep our minds sharp for intellectual discourse, and drugs and alcohol prevented us from remembering the minutia of our conversations. We wanted to be able to pick up our train of thought wherever we left off in the hopes of creating an unbroken chain of topics spiraling out into infinity.

As a magician, you had a few tricks up your sleeve, some of which I discovered later, after we became a couple. First, you financed all of my dates with the Page of Swords, who couldn't find employment beyond the gas station where he worked part-time. For my senior ball, you loaned the Page of Swords enough money to take me to an expensive Italian restaurant in Los Gatos where fresh candles graced the white linen tablecloths and a live band played classical music. Instead of taking your advice and booking the reservation, the Page of Swords took me to a pizza joint and pocketed the difference so he could buy second-hand CDs of Tower of Power and Phil Collins from Amoeba Records in San Francisco. When you heard the news, you grew oddly quiet, even quieter than you normally were. I remember the temperature in the room dropping a few degrees. I shivered, afraid of your silence. I knew you were upset. I just didn't know you weren't upset with me. Second, you gave advice to the Page of Swords when it came to my relationship with him. This fact I discovered when, after a rather blistering argument in which I initiated breaking up for the second time, the Page of Swords swooped in and rescued the situation using a line you had fed him. When I softened, agreeing to give our love one more try, the Page of Swords kissed me and exclaimed, "The Magician was right again!" I felt duped like I was Roxane in *Cyrano de Bergerac*, which, in a sense, I was. Finally, when the Page of Swords invited me to take my youngest sister to Christmas in the Park, you drove all of us in your station wagon, which was fondly referred to as "the hearse," to the winter wonderland where we strolled along the staged scenes from Frosty the Snowman to the Birth of Jesus. When my sister complained her tummy hurt because she was hungry, you paid for her Happy Meal because the Page of Swords had only seventy cents to his name. Afterward, when my sister's legs cramped from too much walking, you hoisted her onto your shoulders, giving her a piggy back ride back to your car. As soon as you dropped us off, my sister turned to me and asked, "Why aren't you dating the Magician?" to which I replied, "Because I am a Fool."

I did wise up a bit after seeking counsel from the trusty tarot. Back then, Laura read my cards. She spread the shuffled deck into a relationship reading and revealed the path I should take with my romantic life.

I remember this reading in particular because I had spent the night in her bedroom at her parents' house. Sleepovers had always been forbidden, but I was eighteen going on nineteen, so my parents didn't protest. I sat cross-legged on her hardwood floor, placing my palms on the backs of the cards, silently asking my question, "Should I stay with my boyfriend, the Page of Swords, or should I date his best friend, the Magician?"

A few events had led up to this quandary, but I will only mention the one that matters—the day I fell in love with you.

On February 11, 1990, you came over to see the Page of Swords. You wanted to talk, but I was there. At first, you thought the two of you were alone. The Page of Swords' big, burly body blocked the doorway. As soon as you stepped into the hallway of his parents' house, you glimpsed me, a wisp of a woman behind him.

You raised your eyebrows and crinkled your forehead.

"I can leave." I waved my hand toward the hallway. "I just need to save my work and get my purse."

At the last moment, you relented. "No, please, stay. I have something for you."

From out of thin air, you produced a long-stemmed chocolate rose the color of my lipstick.

"I made it." You handed me the rose wrapped in clear, plastic cellophane.

Smiling, I twirled the gift between my fingers

and followed you down the hallway to the Page of Swords' bedroom.

The two of you sat on the edge of the bed while I resumed my space in front of the computer, typing the first draft of my memoir about growing up Chinese American in the late seventies. Years later you would tell strangers we met when you rescued my memoir off the failed hard drive of my boyfriend's computer, which is a fact, but not the truth. The truth is I fell in love you with that night, listening to you tell my boyfriend about your struggles to gain the love and affection of the Empress who was dating another man, a woman I had seen in passing but had never met, a woman who I felt did not deserve you.

At one point in the conversation, you slapped your hands against your thighs. "I just want someone to go to the library with."

Library? I stopped typing. I loved to read. My favorite place in the whole world was the library. I even thought about becoming a librarian before a teacher dissuaded me, saying one day the Dewey Decimal System would be completely replaced by computers. I dropped my hands into my lap and swiveled. "I'll go to the library with you."

You lifted your bowed head and met my gaze. "You will?"

I had never seen eyes so blue—electric blue like the song by Icehouse. The lyrics raced through my mind then disappeared. I felt like I was seeing you for the first time—a shy, young man with no self-confidence striving to be loved, accepted, and understood. "Yes, of course, I love the library. When do you want to go?"

You drew a map showing me directions to your house. You wrote your phone number at the top of the page in small, fine print.

The Page of Swords observed this interaction without comment.

When I glanced down at my watch, I gasped. Fifteen minutes to get home before my curfew. With trembling hands, I gathered my belongings, folding the map and tucking it inside my purse next to the long-stemmed chocolate rose.

You and the Page of Swords walked me to my car parked along the street.

I opened the passenger door and tossed my purse on the seat.

"May I have a hug?" You approached me with your arms wide open.

My father taught me to always hug everyone hello and goodbye. But your request caught me by surprise. Before tonight you had always shied away, refusing to be touched. I stepped around the bushes next to the curb, back onto the sidewalk, and into your embrace. I squeezed you tight, flattening my breasts against your chest, patting my hands against your back. You smelled of fried fish from working at Tom and Jerry's and bergamot and mandarin from your signature cologne. The dark night enveloped us. The air was as warm and comforting as friendship. The rush of traffic on the busy street sounded like background music.

For a long moment, neither one of us wanted to let go.

Remembering that night and everything that transpired since, I closed my eyes and placed my hands on the tarot cards and asked the question burning in my soul—should I stay with the Page of Swords or leave for the Magician?

Laura read the interpretations of the cards from a book, adding her own insight into the process. She revealed the first card. "One of the men is full of intellect. But he is all talk and no action. He will promise, but not deliver." She flipped over the next card. "The other man is full of mastery. He says what he means. He delivers what he promises." She frowned. "Do you know who these men are?"

I nodded. The first man was the Page of Swords. The second man was the Magician.

She continued with the reading. "You have always followed your head." With her long fingers, she caressed the card full of swords before flipping over the next card full of cups. "But you need to follow your heart this time." She turned over the final card and smiled. "In listening to your heart, you will know which man to choose." She blinked back tears of joy. "His love will transform you."

I stared at the overturned cards and nodded. The decision was self-evident. I would break up with the Page of Swords. I would date the Magician. I would let my life be transformed.

∼

THE NEXT CARD IN THE CELTIC CROSS READING represents one's psychological state during the time of the question. Under certain circumstances, the physiological state should be included, since one's body is closely linked to one's mind. I draw yet another Major Arcana card, The Hierophant, which typically repre-

sents traditional beliefs and customs. The image on the card features the pope sitting between dual pillars with two monks at his feet. The Hierophant reflects humankind's historical attempt to understand and explain the mystery of existence through organized religion and tradition. When this card is selected, one is likely to conform to convention rather than risk acting on one's individual beliefs which might contradict the standards of society.

∾

LOUISE LAPE, A TAROT READER AND MEDIUM, SAYS, "Once I read for my friend who asked when she would meet a man. When I said, 'Soon,' she asked, 'How soon?' I drew another card and said, 'Very soon. Looks like either two days or two weeks.' She called me up three days later and said, 'I met the man.' They've been married for several years now."

As the days pass, I wonder why I didn't ask Melanie for a specific date when I would get the new job or meet the man who would heal my heart.

I continue to go on job interviews. I continue to pray. I continue to have faith in the prediction.

One month after the tarot reading with Melanie, I receive a generous offer to work at a community bank. On the first day of work, I am introduced to all of the employees. Each time I shake a man's hand, I wonder, "Are you the man who will heal my heart?" Not feeling the spark of recognition from any of the men, I go home and think about Melanie's prediction—one out of two isn't bad.

~

WE WORK ON OUR MARRIAGE. THROUGH COUPLE'S counseling, I discover I do not understand your love language. You give gifts to show your affection—bouquets of fragrant roses from a roadside floral stand, rich and creamy specialty chocolates, and homemade bath bombs that smell like a tropical garden of birds of paradise and coconut milk. When I don't properly acknowledge your gifts, you feel rejected. The gifts stop, and love dries up.

You rediscover I need words of love to fill me. You start to write me letters every day to share your thoughts and feelings.

We learn about attachment styles formed from our childhoods. We pin a diagram on the bulletin board in the home office we share and point to the fears that keep us apart whenever we start to argue. We are supposed to strip naked when we fight, but we can't. Our arguments always arise as soon as you step through the front door, and our children are awake. Forever Child, our fifteen-year-old disabled son, roams the house, looking for food we've hidden so he does not eat until he throws up. Princess Pea, our ten-year-old daughter, needs help with homework. She struggles with an auditory processing disorder and a slight case of dyslexia. There is no time for us.

My anxieties rise and fall like unpredictable tides, but no one mentions the one thing these uncontrollable rhythms might be linked to—peri-menopause.

I am ten years away from the moment I will start skipping periods on the eventual road toward menopause, but my body has begun to change now. I am a teenager in reverse. Instead of my body ramping up with estrogen and progesterone to produce offspring, my body is downshifting, getting ready to coast into the final stage of being a woman. No one—not my general practitioner, our marriage counselor, our priest, or family and friends—mentions this variable to our problems. How can they? My doctor thinks I am too young. Our marriage counselor is clueless. Our priest has never lived with a woman. Our friends are too busy trying to disentangle their own knotted lives. Both of our mothers had hysterectomies at a younger age. They never entered this danger zone.

I feel so isolated with my symptoms, but I am not alone. According to Lynda Wisdo, author of *Menopause in Crisis: When Spiritual Emergency Meets the Feminine Midlife Passage*, fifteen to twenty percent of women experience such intense physical and emotional turmoil they fear they are losing their minds.

I haven't tipped into that perilous territory yet, but my libido rises and falls erratically, sending us both into a tailspin. Do I ask for sex or do I wait? Sometimes when you are tired, having stayed awake with our Forever Child until 4 AM, you only want to sleep. How can you tactfully tell me to place my hormonal needs aside? You are tired. You are grumpy. Your batteries are so low you can barely crawl into the queen-sized bed before you collapse into sleep.

Other times, I am moody. Not the predictable moods of a regular hormonal cycle, but the staggered rise and dip of someone suffering from a mental illness. I want to be held tight. I want to be left alone. I want to scream. I want to whisper. I want to leave the family and never return. I want to stay home in bed, curled up beneath the covers, and never leave the safety of these four walls. Sometimes I do not know what I want or need anymore.

Over the course of our therapy sessions, the therapist weaves a narrative, linking our different personalities into an inevitable tragedy. "He's a wild stallion who needs his freedom," the therapist says about you. "Don't fence him into your marriage with your outdated rules about fidelity and loyalty. He knows the boundaries. He just wants to enjoy the view unfettered from his position. Caging him into your relationship will only force him to jump the fence so he can feel the freedom he deserves."

The medication prescribed to help my moods flattens my ability to feel and function. I walk around in a hazy fog of uncaring, performing everything by rote. The emotional outbursts flat line, which seems ideal at first, until the husk of the woman in your living room can no longer love anyone. She is as caring as a robot.

All of this therapy and medication does nothing but elevate the conflict between us. Now we have stones we can throw at each other during a fight.

"You're a wild animal, not a civilized man!"

"You're a crazy bitch, not a normal woman!"

Neither accusation is right.

Eventually, we stop counseling after the push-pull dynamic escalates, leaving us both exhausted and alone.

I discontinue the prescription medication and try some over-the-counter remedies instead. I find some relief in 5-HTP, which smoothes out my sleep, levels out my moods, and increases my creativity and caring.

You agree to reduce the amount of time you devote to your business and increase the amount of time you devote to me.

Together, we ride out the challenges on our own. We love each other, after all. Eighteen years ago, we received the Sacrament of Marriage in the Catholic Church with over one hundred family and friends as witnesses. We've endured the struggles of raising a child with developmental delay, seizures, cerebral palsy, and autism. We've powered through the ups and downs of job losses, abortion, miscarriage, infidelity (both real and imagined), and addictions (porn—yours, food and alcohol—mine). We've sacrificed for ambition—your computer repair business and my art and writing. Why can't we get through whatever demons remain between us?

∾

A YEAR LATER, WHILE I AM BUSYING GATHERING loan documents from a printer, I glance up and notice a fellow co-worker escorting the new hire down the hallway. The new hire is a tall, trim man dressed in a burgundy dress shirt and black slacks. A soft, warm glow fills my chest. *That's him. That's the man who will heal my heart.* I smile, marveling at how lucky I am to be paired up with such a good-looking man.

That night, after our children are asleep, I sit on the black ottoman while you work on your laptop. I fold my trembling hands into my lap and steady my voice. "Today I met the man who will heal my heart."

You continue typing without raising your head.

I sigh. Maybe you forgot about the tarot reading. After all, the prediction happened almost a year ago. Why would you remember?

Leaning forward, I clasp my hands between my knees. Worry knits my forehead. I remember walking into the Knight of Cups' office to introduce myself, since I missed the formal introductions earlier in the day. Standing in the doorway, I hesitated. He hunched over an open loan file, intently reading. The light from the window behind him illuminated his body like a giant, golden halo. I wanted to extend my hand and say, "Hi, I'm your future wife," but I remembered reading a story about Michael Douglas almost ruining his chances with Catherine Zeta-Jones when he said, "You know, I'm going to be the father of your children," and decided not to scare away this stranger. After taking a deep breath, I gave the Knight of Cups my legal name and my department title, nothing more and nothing less. I'm glad I did, because when I shook his hand and listened to him rattle off his resume of prior banking experience, I knew he had no clue about the future between us.

I shift on the ottoman, needing to convey the significance of this event. "Remember when I saw that tarot reader last year?"

You nod, still typing.

"Well, she drew the Knight of Cups from her tarot deck and predicted I would get a job and meet a man there who would heal my heart." I smooth my hands against my jeans and take another breath. "Well, I got the job at the bank, but I didn't meet anyone who would heal my heart, so I thought the tarot reader only got one out of the two predictions right." I shift my hips and study the tiny computer screen reflected in your reading glasses. "What I didn't know is he wasn't working at the bank when I was hired. I just assumed the predictions had to occur at the same time. But I was wrong, and she was right. I met the man at work today."

You stop typing, raise your chin, and lock your gaze with mine. "What are you saying?"

I am calm and poised like I am in front of a podium delivering a speech I memorized. "I met my second husband today."

You swallow and your blue eyes widen, but you don't say a word.

All the years crash around us—the whirlwind romance when I left the Page of Swords to date you, our move from Silicon Valley to Sonoma County to start a new life away from our families, the unplanned pregnancy ending in an abortion, the ultimatum leading to our marriage, the work injury and job rehabilitation, the graduation from college, the birth of our Forever Child, the teeter totter between fidelity and infidelity, the descent into grief and alcoholism, the closet pornography, the birth of our Princess Pea, the years of staying sober, staying present, staying vigilant only to dead end with this prophecy's fruition.

You snap shut your laptop and bristle. "Are you saying we should get a divorce?"

I shrug. I still do not see how this whole series of events will manifest. I only know what happened today. I met the Knight of Cups, the man who would heal my heart. He is my future husband. The rest of the details—how we will go from strangers to a couple—are not revealed to me. Those details I must live out just like the rest of us.

∿

THE NEXT CARD IN THE CELTIC CROSS READING REFERS to my environment and any unforeseen forces beyond my control. I draw another Major Arcana card, The Chariot. The image of a man in a cube-like carriage drawn by two sphinx-like animals puzzles me. The Chariot typically indicates swift movement in a new direction, sometimes through physical travel. But I have not gone anywhere or done anything. Four uneventful years have passed since I met the man who will heal my heart. Our marriage has never been better. I am happy. You love me with the same patient devotion of our early days together. Our children are doing well in their lives. Our son attends the best school for students with developmental disabilities and our daughter has just entered high school with the ease she lacked transitioning from elementary to middle school. My memoir, which I began writing at eighteen, has won the She Writes Press Memoir Discovery Contest and will be published in October 2015. Furthermore, the job I have at the bank sufficiently pays all of our bills and provides health insurance for the entire family. You are free to work at your leisure, building your computer business while caring for our children. I have no desire to suddenly change directions or travel. How can this card be right?

~

NOTHING STAYS THE SAME. THAT'S THE NATURE OF impermanence. I am not a Buddhist, but I am aware of change. First, the air thins. I take three breaths to equal one. Next, the earth shifts, not suddenly like an earthquake, but gently like an invisible slope, rising millimeter by millimeter, so by the time I reach the top and turn around, the bottom has fallen away completely, and I am somewhere else.

In January, a mysterious white and gray rabbit shows up in our driveway during one of my early morning runs. Every day for the next two weeks, this lost bunny greets me. Sometimes you and our children glimpse its presence in the grass beside the chain link fence or hopping away to a neighbor's yard. Our daughter, Princess Pea, and I decide to name the bunny Fifer after the psychic bunny in *Watership Down*. You tease us, calling the bunny Michelle Pfeiffer, instead.

One morning, when I leave for my early morning run, I do not see Fifer hunched in the gutter. I do not see it nibbling grass or hopping along the sidewalk. It is gone. For days, we search the neighborhood looking for the mysterious bunny. When we cannot find it, we assume it has found its way back home.

~

A WEEK LATER, I AM AT WORK SITTING IN THE conference room with the bank president, the Knight of Cups, and a famous vintner who has come to us for a loan.

The tall, gangly, and elderly vintner frowns and waves a hand over the loan documents I am here to notarize. "My property appraised much higher than I anticipated. May I withdraw more funds? Say another million or two?"

The bank president adjusts his aviator sunglasses on the crown of his brown hair and raises his eyebrows.

The Knight of Cups, who is the vintner's loan officer, nods. He is wearing the same burgundy shirt and black slacks he wore the day I first met him. Crow's feet crease the corners of his blue eyes. When he smiles, an old scar on his chin forms a dimple. His long hands and graceful fingers shuffle through a stack of papers. "I think I could underwrite the loan for two million. I'll call you next week, and let you know."

The vintner leans back against the chair and smiles, flashing his gleaming white dentures. "Could you also come to my home? The trip to town is hard on my bones."

The bank president gestures his arm wide. "I'm sure we can accommodate you."

A home visit? I frown and glance over at the Knight of Cups.

He shrugs and flashes a crooked smile.

Heat dances across my face before plunging through my chest and settling in my lap. The atoms of fate zing in the electricity powering the air. I twist my hands in my lap. The gravitational pull of destiny tugs the soles of my feet through my black flats. I curl my toes and resist. After all, I love being married to you. I love our family. I love the life I have created.

Sweat dampens my forehead. I glance around the table at the tired, wizened face of the old vintner, at the reflection from the fluorescent lights against the bank president's sunglasses, and the Knight of Cups' long fingers twirling a silver pen like a miniature baton. I clench my jaw and ball my hands into fists. At this moment, I decide to intervene in the power of predestination. I will refuse to accompany the Knight of Cups to the vintner's home in Sonoma, so I can stop destiny and save my beloved family, including us.

After the meeting, I wave to the Knight of Cups. "I can't leave the department for a signing at the vintner's home. Please find another notary."

"No problem." With a quick nod, he leaves.

I exhale with relief. *That was easy. See, free will does exist.*

A week before the appointment, the Knight of Cups emails me.

—*No other notary is available.*—

I stare at the cursor blinking like an insouciant eye. With trembling fingers, I tap the keys.

—I already told you I can't go. I need to stay and take care of my department.—

Ten minutes later, my boss calls me into her office.

After I close the door and take a seat across from her desk, she frowns. "Why did you say you're unavailable to notarize documents? Don't you know I can manage the department while you're away?"

I lean forward, my hips barely on the chair. "I don't want to go and lose my marriage."

She laughs, tossing back her head, her mouth open so wide I can count her silver fillings.

No amount of explaining about fate and destiny and tarot readings will convince my boss I'm not crazy. I feel boxed in, trapped with no escape.

When you get home that night, I corner you at the front door. "I need your help."

You drop your computer bag at your feet and cross your arms over your chest. "What did we learn in therapy?"

I can't believe you're mentioning therapy in the midst of a family emergency. I throw up my arms. "Don't talk to you immediately when you get home. Give you ten minutes to settle." I step back and pace, a caged animal on death row. "If you don't help me, then all is lost."

Frowning, you grip my shoulders and pull me toward your chest.

I rest my forehead on your collar bone and sob. "I don't want to go to Sonoma next week. I don't want to notarize the loan documents. I don't want to spend three hours alone with the Knight of Cups." I sniff, twisting out of your arms. "Can't you work your magic and make this business transaction disappear?" I glance up at the ceiling, thinking. "The vintner is old. Maybe you could wave your wand and make him sick so he has to go to the hospital and never return."

You stare blankly at me.

I wave my arms like rainfall. "Maybe you could send a flood and wipe out the vineyards so the bank will not consummate the loan since there will be no collateral."

You slowly shake your head.

With the back of my hand, I swipe the tears off my cheeks. "Then let me quit my job and save our marriage."

You laugh. "I can't support us. I can barely support my business." You sink into your black armchair, heave a sigh, and rub your forehead. "What are you afraid of?"

"The future." I perch on the black ottoman, hands clasped between my knees, my gaze fixed on the laminate flooring. "I don't want to lose *us*."

"Then don't." Your voice is firm, resolute, the final answer. You stand, grab your computer bag, and stalk to the home office. You close the door and turn up the volume of your music.

Our son, Forever Child, wanders down the hallway. He is as short as me and as lean as a steel beam. He pauses at the ledge between the dining area and the living room and opens his mouth to form one of the few words he can speak. "Eat."

Sighing, I rise and stride into the kitchen to

make dinner. My pulse ticks like a timed bomb. The air is thin. The earth is crumbly. Change has already started. Its engine revs, shifts, propels us forward. I am powerless to stop it.

～

ON THE MORNING OF THE TRIP, I STAND IN THE bank's parking lot and squint at the blue winter sky. The sun is unusually bright and warm for January. I strip out of my black business jacket and climb into the Knight of Cups' pickup truck. I tug the seatbelt across my lap, fold my jacket over the notary bag, and wait.

The Knight of Cups turns the key in the ignition. He shifts the gear into reverse and backs out of the slot then shifts into drive and lumbers into traffic.

During the forty-five minute drive, no one talks.

As soon as we arrive, the old vintner waves us across the grand stone entryway. "Let me give you a tour."

We spend a half hour wandering around the mansion. The old vintner narrates from room to room like a tour guide. We examine the black and white photographs of Italy haunting the dark, formal dining room. We admire the big game trophies on the twenty-foot walls in the light-filled great room. We gaze in wonder at the inky black infinity pool in the backyard overlooking hundreds of acres of vineyards. Finally, we settle at the breakfast bar in the granite and stainless steel kitchen to go over the loan and sign the documents.

Afterward, the old vintner shakes our hands goodbye.

I sigh with relief. Nothing bad happened. No energy shifted in the universe. The future didn't collapse around us.

After setting the notary bag at my feet, I tug the seatbelt over my lap and prop my elbow on the ledge of the passenger's window. I feel safe enough for small talk. Since I don't know much about him, I decide to ask about his family. "So, how are your kids?"

As he drives, the Knight of Cups slaps the steering wheel. "Why does everyone always ask about the kids?"

The hot venom in his voice splatters me. I wince.

He grips the steering wheel. "How come no one asks about me?"

I gulp, surprised by the sudden outburst of emotion. Tentatively, I direct the conversation back to him. "How are *you* doing?"

Without looking at me, he dips his chin toward his chest. "I wanted to be a firefighter when I was younger, but I'm too old now." He relaxes his grip on the steering wheel.

Too old? I shift toward him. "I know a guy in his fifties who volunteers."

He shakes his head. "I want a new career, not another hobby."

Bowing my head, I lace my fingers together in my lap and think.

"I've been divorced for ten years." He lifts a

hand from the steering wheel and massages his forehead. "I don't know what color to paint my family room. I haven't been with a woman." He lifts one shoulder with a sigh. "I mean—I've dated."

I nod, understanding the subtext. "But you haven't found anyone special." *Until me*. The phrase floats from the depths of my subconscious to the surface of my thoughts. The only thing stopping me from uttering the words is my teeth are clenched tighter than my fists. *Did he hear me thinking?* Wary, I glance at his profile.

He stares ahead and steers into the parking lot. After he turns off the engine, he unleashes his seatbelt and props open the door. A cool breeze floats through the cab. "Are you coming?" His gaze is soft and blue like the sky.

I slip out of the truck and tug my arms through the black jacket. The sun is still bright and the sky is still clear, but the air is thick and cold with winter.

A slight shudder ripples throughout my body, and the nerves in my hands and feet tingle.

I grab my notary bag in one hand, my purse in the other and match his pace, stride for stride, across the blacktop toward the glass and steel building.

The veil between the present and the future floats between us.

At the double doors, he stops and turns toward me. "Just forget about that conversation we had, okay? You have a family. You don't need to worry about my life."

But suddenly I am thinking about his life— from his thwarted ambitions to the shape and size of his family room to the dizzying sizzle between us.

"Okay, but I read a lot about people in midlife reinventing their careers. If I see something of interest, may I forward it to you?"

For a long moment, he gazes into my eyes, and the whole world pivots in the wrong direction. The veil between what was and what will be flutters, and I wonder which one of us will be the first to cross to the other side.

"Sure." He ushers me into the building. "I trust your judgment."

I swallow and blink, the statement settling like a brick at the bottom of my stomach. How can he trust my judgment? He doesn't know me. I don't know him. We are strangers walking in a strange land with no one to guide us.

~

The next card in the Celtic Cross reading references the state of my relationship with others. I draw the Seven of Swords, which generally refers to lies and tricks and possible dishonesty. I wonder about how honest I've been with others and how honest others have been with me. But I don't stop to think about how honest I've been with myself.

~

In the New Testament of the Bible, Peter, Jesus' most loyal disciple, swears he will always acknowledge his affiliation with him, no matter the circumstance. However, Jesus predicts Peter will deny him three times before the rooster crows. Later that night, Jesus is betrayed by another one of his disciples, Judas, in exchange for thirty pieces of silver. After Jesus' arrest by the Romans, Peter and some of the other disciples see if they can find someone in power who will release Jesus. While Peter waits to speak with the High Priest, a girl at the gates asks Peter if he is one of Jesus' disciples. He says no. Another person waiting to speak with the High Priest asks Peter if he is one of Jesus' disciples. Again, he says no. Finally, one of the High Priest's slaves recognizes him. "Didn't I see you with Jesus in the garden before his arrest?" For a third time, he says no. Immediately, thereafter, a rooster crows, and Peter is filled with guilt and remorse.

Like Peter, I deny you three times.

Like Peter, I am filled with guilt and remorse.

How did this happen?

Could it have been prevented?

Like Jesus' prophesy, I don't think so.

The first time I deny you I am sitting on the black leather sofa in the remodeled living room sketching greeting cards with watercolor pencils while you and Princess Pea watch the latest episode of "Ghost Hunters" on TV. I am creating a thank you card for the bank's receptionist who bought the watercolor pencils for me. The colors blend beautifully with a brush dipped in water. Swirls of pink and lavender petals blossom into a bouquet that will never wilt or decay.

Next, I create a card for the Knight of Cups. After our trip to the vintner's house in January, we have kept the conversation between us flowing.

Every day he emails me about what's happening in his life, from his troubles with his teenage children to his mother's sudden illness that landed her in the ICU. I respond with tidbits of my life, from my challenges balancing work and writing to my adventures with my husband and children. On Monday mornings, I bring the extra coffee cake to the office and leave it on his desk. He surprises me with gifts he receives from his clients but cannot use: a pound of gourmet coffee beans for me, a dozen gluten-free, dairy-free cupcakes from the new locally owned bakery for my children, and tickets to Sonoma Raceway for my husband. A friendship has taken root between us. I sketch a path through a forest. Several leaves fall on the winding trail. Everything is black and white except for a single, red, heart-shaped leaf off in the distance. Inside, I write, "Thank you for bringing color into my life." I sign the salutation, "Your friend, the Fool." I do not think about the irony of this situation—I've become what I detest—a woman who gives a man who does not belong to her a greeting card. Furthermore, the card is also reminiscent of the first greeting card you gave me almost twenty-five years ago. On the front cover of your greeting card, a small, red heart with a tiny smile graced the white expanse. Inside, the message read, "That's all I had to say."

Right now, as I am drawing, I am not thinking of the woman who gave you a greeting card almost five years ago. I am not remembering the first greeting card you gave me. I am not thinking at all. I am moving the pencil over the paper, creating another world in which I will escape.

On Valentine's Day, I send an email to the Knight of Cups. "Do you have any lunch plans?"

Within minutes, he responds. "No. Where do you want to go?"

I suggest Brody's, my favorite burger joint, which is a five-minute drive from the office.

At noon, we meet in the bank's parking lot. The sky is clear and bright for February. I offer to drive. Scooting the passenger seat completely back, I hope there is enough room for him since he is over six feet tall. He crouches inside my tiny vehicle and doesn't say much on the drive. I roll down the window and let the cool, dry air whip across my face. What a remarkable winter day in wine country.

Inside the diner, the heat and sizzle from the grills mingle with the nervous perspiration dotting my forehead.

He glances at the prices on the overhead menu and reaches for his wallet. "I'm paying."

I widen my stance. "But I asked you out."

"You have a family." He removes a wad of cash.

"So do you." I shove my hand into my purse.

He waves away my gesture. "I make more than you do."

The truth darts at my ego, and I zip up my purse, surrendering.

We find a table with chairs as high as bar stools toward the back of the diner next to the floor-to-ceiling windows. So much light streams through, illuminating everything from the errant crumb on the red table to the lines etched inside my palms. I feel luminescent, bathed in so much sunshine, and

I smile, remembering your term of endearment for me, "Sun Bunny."

But this memory evaporates as soon as our number is called.

He leaves to retrieve the tray of burgers, fries, and drinks.

As I watch him weave around customers to the front counter, I feel something different about this lunch over all the other lunches we've shared. I shift against the bar stool and crumple a paper napkin in my hand. Heat radiates from the center of me. This lunch is a date, our first date, on Valentine's Day. Guilt weaves up my ankles and curls at the bottom of my stomach. Inside my purse, the homemade card pulses like a heartbeat.

One moment of clarity rises like steam.

I can keep the card.

I can bow my head, eat the burger and fries, and pretend I have no other motive.

When he returns, he removes the items from the tray and sets them on the table. The scent of salty fries wafts between us.

He misinterprets my shame-stained face. "I'm sorry I forgot the ketchup." Turning, he leaves for the front counter.

My gaze travels after him, caressing the glossy sheen of his brown hair to the expanse of his broad back to the narrows of his waist to his full, tight buttocks. At work, I sit near the aisle and track his movements up and down the hallway several times a day. My gaze always follows the same pattern, zigzagging across his tall, trim body.

When he returns, he hunches his shoulders.

"You know that article you gave me about a month ago?"

I nod, recalling the personal reinvention stories of other middle-aged men and women who left their jobs to pursue outside interests.

He sighs. "I don't have a passion that translates into a career at this late date." He spreads his empty hands. "I'm over fifty. I can't play professional baseball." He grimaces and curls a hand into a fist. "I should have applied to be a firefighter when I was thirty-five, but I didn't. I was too caught up in my family's drama and later my divorce." He glances across the room. "I think I should just look forward to retirement." He nods. "That would suit me."

A soft pain throbs in my chest. I have passions, lots of them, and I follow them wherever they lead me—running in races, painting landscapes, creating greeting cards, teaching scrapbooking to children, instructing adults on how to use fiction techniques to write their memoirs, and writing and publishing books. I can't imagine not running and reading and painting and teaching and writing. How barren my life would be if I did not pursue what brings me joy on a daily basis.

Without thinking, I plunge my hand into my purse and remove the homemade greeting card. "I have something for you." I slide the envelope across the table. "Happy Valentine's Day."

He takes the cream-colored envelope into his hands. Carefully, he breaks the seal and withdraws the card. He stares at the picture for a long moment before he opens the card. As he reads the words, the expression on his face changes. The muscles around his mouth relax. "Thank you." He tucks the card into his breast pocket and meets my gaze. "I can't believe you made this for me." A smile lingers in his blue eyes.

After lunch, I drive back to the bank and park.

He steps out of the vehicle and pats his chest where the card rests. "Thank you again."

"You're welcome." I smile, feeling ten pounds lighter.

We walk side by side across the parking lot. The sky is still blue and clear. The air is still warm and dry. A typical winter day in Northern California, but the seeds of denial have been planted in our hearts.

~

THE SECOND TIME I FORGET I AM MARRIED HAPPENS a month later during a business trip to Los Angeles. Brenda, my boss, reconnects with an old friend, Frank, during the conference, and after a full day of seminars, the three of us head out to Manhattan Beach for sightseeing and dinner. Inside Rock 'N Fish Steak and Seafood, away from the loud bar and the kaleidoscope of stained glass mermaids, I sit in a booth across from Brenda and Frank and browse the menu. The scents of fried fish and tangy drinks fill the sultry air.

After ordering crab cakes, I take out my phone. Every year I miss our daughter's birthday for a business trip. Every year I buy her a present in the airport terminal—sweatshirts with the names of the cities I visit. She wears them with pride, telling others about the places she's never been, the places only I have traveled. Deep down, she misses me. She wishes I didn't have to work on her birthday. She would prefer to sit across from me at the kitchen table blowing out candles on a gluten-free, dairy-free cake I baked. Today she is fifteen. I find her number.

—*Happy Birthday, Princess Pea! Wish I was there. Here's a picture of the beach.*—

I attach a photograph I took earlier in the evening of the gray water lapping against the beige sand.

When she doesn't respond, I assume she is celebrating with you and her brother.

Your number is the first in my list of contacts. Warm gratitude fills my chest. I quickly type you a text.

—*Thank you for taking care of our family. I miss you guys. Please let Princess Pea know I sent her a text wishing her a happy birthday.*—

I know you will be too busy with the children to respond until later that night as I am lying in bed, trying to sleep.

Brenda nudges Frank, laughing at some inside joke. Their intimacy shoots off sparks, a firework celebration in the middle of spring.

A chill rushes up my arms, and I drop my phone into my lap and rub my skin until it warms.

My phone chimes.

I swipe my finger across the screen, and an image of Princess Pea blowing out the candles on her cake blooms.

Smiling, I feel the sunshine of your love power through me.

—*Thank you for sending this picture.*—

For a long moment, I think about attaching a picture of the beach. But then I wonder if you will feel as lonely as I do. I don't want to hurt you anymore than I already have by my absence, so I press Send without an image.

Brenda and Frank giggle, petting each other's arms.

I bristle. *Why don't I have a work friend cuddling next to me?* Scowling, I scroll through my contacts and find the Knight of Cups' phone number. I don't have a photograph from the lending seminar from earlier in the day, so I attach a photograph of Manhattan Beach, the same one I sent to my daughter.

—*Wish you were here.*—

After I press Send, I cup the phone in my lap and wait.

Brenda and Frank reminisce and gossip about their lives. They met while working at a commercial bank in San Diego where Brenda lived during her first marriage. Frank was a member of her loan documentation team. On weekends, Frank would babysit Brenda's children so she could go to dinner and a movie with her then-husband. Eventually, Brenda divorced and moved north to Sonoma County. But the two of them have kept in touch for over twenty years.

A few moments later, my phone vibrates against my thighs. I swipe my finger across the screen and read the Knight of Cups' response.

—*This must be for your husband. You sent it to me by mistake.*—

Heat invades my face. I grip the phone tighter, wondering how I should respond.

Brenda and Frank chat, unaware of the dangerous stick of dynamite in my hand.

My heartbeat stomps up and down the staircase of my body. *Think, think, think.* An old feeling of dread from one-sided love fills each breath I take. I could back pedal and mention the work conference, waiting for dinner with my boss and her friend, and how I wish he was here, sitting beside me, talking about the client with the billboards as collateral for a loan. But I don't. Sidestepping the dilemma, I toss the problem in his direction.

—*Did I?*—

I drop the heated phone in my lap. I smile at a joke Brenda makes. When my phone chimes again, I glance down at the message.

—*I would love to walk barefoot with you along the beach.*—

A huge smile dawns on my face. Every inch of my skin tingles.

The server brings fried calamari and cocktail sauce. The grease sizzles in the air.

Brenda and Frank stop talking. They unfurl their white napkins and dig into the calamari.

—*Just sat down to dinner, talk to you later.*—

—*Work isn't the same without you. Have a good night.*—

I tuck the phone into my purse and wipe my sweaty palms on the cloth napkin. I dip a hot, crisp calamari into the tangy cocktail sauce and chew the tender insides.

After dinner, while Brenda, Frank, and I stroll along the balmy streets toward the shuttle that will take us back to the hotel, I see a mannequin wearing the perfect T-shirt in the storefront window of a closed shop. I pause and take a snapshot with my phone's camera. The message on the simple, white T-shirt reads, "You look a lot like my next boyfriend." Although I feel that way about the Knight of Cups, I do not send him the picture. Some things I keep safe, close to my heart, a secret I will not share with anyone, even if they ask.

~

TEN DAYS LATER, WHILE I AM EATING DINNER WITH you and our children on a Saturday night, my cell phone chimes in the living room.

We have always had a policy of no phones, no TV, and no music, at the dinner table. In spite of our busy schedules, we hold Saturdays sacred, from morning car washing and coffee cake to afternoon grocery shopping to evening Mass followed by a home cooked meal.

Everyone who knows our family doesn't contact us on Saturdays unless it is an emergency.

As soon as Princess Pea places her dishes in the sink and disappears to finish homework in her bedroom and Forever Child lumbers down the hall to listen to grunge music in his bedroom, you box up the leftovers while I retrieve my cell phone from the black lacquered end table in the living room. I carry the phone into the kitchen where the scent of grilled chicken, steamed vegetables, and brown rice hangs heavy in the warm, still air. I swipe the screen and an image of the Knight of Cups pops up. I hold my breath. *What does he want?* Dampness soaks the back of my neck. I glance up at you carrying dishes to the sink. A jackknife springs open in my chest. *Can your magical powers see through the lies I tell myself?*

You stack the plates on the counter and turn on the water.

I exhale slowly, and the jackknife snaps shut.

You do not know the Knight of Cups and I have been texting after work every day since the business conference in Los Angeles. *Should I have told you? What difference would it have made?* After all, the Knight of Cups and I only discuss work and our families. And we have never contacted each other on the weekends—until now.

"Who is it?" You turn off the water and dry your hands on a dishtowel. Furrows deepen across your forehead. "Is it an emergency?"

Your gaze is concerned and loving. With quivering hands, I cup the phone and silently read the message.

—*I was at an auction and I bid on something for you. I'll bring it to work on Monday.*—

My eyes widen, and I drop the phone against the kitchen table.

"What happened?" You dash over and touch my shoulder. "Are your parents all right?"

My father has Parkinson's. My mother has arthritis. They both have high blood pressure and high cholesterol. They live over one hundred miles away. But I have two sisters who live close to them. If anything was wrong with my parents, one of them would have alerted me first.

"They're fine." I pick up the phone and swallow my surprise. "The Knight of Cups was at a work function. He bid on something and won. He wants to give it to me on Monday." I frown, handing over my phone to you. The act of surrender absolves me of everything I have neglected to tell you— about the business trip to the vintners in January, about the homemade greeting card in February, about the texting in March. A knot of worry tightens in my lower back. "Why would he bid on something for me?"

You squint, read the message, and shrug. "I don't know. Why don't you ask him what it is?"

I type the message, hit Send, and wait.

A few moments later, my phone chimes.

I swipe the screen and silently read the response.

—*It's a surprise. I hope you like it.*—

After tucking the phone into my front pocket, I join you at the kitchen sink. "He says it's a surprise."

"Then don't worry about it." You squirt floral-smelling dish soap on a sponge.

But I do worry. Anxiety braids up the backs of my legs. I hope the gift isn't jewelry. I roll up my sleeves and rinse the suds from a clean plate with warm water. One year, my best friend, Scott, noticed my admiration of a diamond tennis bracelet in a display case while we were window shopping. He purchased it as a Christmas gift for me, and his wife was jealous. Even I cringed with concern. Jewelry wasn't a gift given between friends. It was reserved for lovers.

Trying not to think about the mystery present, I dry the dishes and stack them in the cupboards. You and I do not talk, although there is plenty to discuss. Next month you are leaving for a business trip to Phoenix, Arizona. You have already told me about your plans to visit the Empress, a woman you first met in high school, the same one you were pining for the day I fell in love with you. The Empress is happily married and a stay-at-home mom to two teenage children. Why should I be worried? You are with me. We have been married for twenty-three years. But. I. Am. Worried. Deep down, I know you have never stopped loving her. Why else would you keep the stuffed bear she bought you for your sixteenth birthday, the year before I met you?

In 2011, a year after I started working at the bank, we drove to visit her family in Tempe, Arizona. I sat in the hotel room with our children, watching movies on the TV, while you helped her prepare for her son's middle school graduation party. A week after we returned from the vacation, I clicked on an email the Empress sent to our family account and discovered photos of her dressed in lingerie. You later explained she had taken those photos for her husband but, as her friend, she wanted your opinion. Were they good enough to give to her husband as a birthday gift or should she get them retaken? I let go of the incident, not wanting to spark any more conflict than I could handle. After all, I had male friends, and I had male lovers. Who was I to judge?

But the hurt ran deep, leaving fissures in the foundation of our marriage.

By the time Monday rolls around, I am full of anxiety.

The Knight of Cups strides down the hallway.

"I have something for you," he says as he passes my desk.

After waiting a respectable amount of time, I log off my computer and stride into his office.

He stands and hands me a shirt-sized box.

"You're giving it to me here?" I glance around nervously at the window behind him and the window behind me. No one is peering inside. No one sees us. But we are close to the file room, a place of heavy foot traffic.

He frowns, holding the box in his hands. "I'll meet you outside by my truck in ten minutes, okay?"

Will the parking lot be any safer?

I glance around one more time before I nod and leave.

What is in that shirt-sized box?

Back in my corner, I read the set of loan documents I'm supposed to review, but the words blur into an inky mush. I stare at the clock on my computer screen, counting down the minutes.

Outside, a blast of warm air brushes my cheeks. I inhale deeply, glancing around the parking lot. A couple of rows away, I glimpse him leaning against the tailgate of his pickup truck. I don't see the shirt-sized box. Exhaling, I stalk over to him. The clip-clop of my heels against the blacktop ticks like a time bomb.

When he sees me, he stands and reaches into the cargo bed. He lifts the box and places it into my hands.

I fidget with the lid.

A black and white striped sweater blows up in my face.

"You're a size small, right?"

Nodding, I hold up the sweater against my chest.

"I thought it would look good on you, all those stripes hugging your curves." He gestures with his hands, making an hour-glass shape.

Heat rushes to my face. The knit material is rough and scratchy. The black cowl neck hangs like a ruffled clown collar. The bell-shaped sweater flares against my hips. The three-quarter length sleeves expose my small wrists. I would never buy something this garish. I swallow, hoping he doesn't expect me to wear this sweater in public. "Thank you."

"Oh, and there's a bracelet." He grabs the box and rummages through the tissue paper and removes a black metal bracelet. He clasps it around my tiny wrist.

The cold metal coils like a black snake. It's as ugly as the sweater, but it is a piece of jewelry just like I feared. I stare at the swirling handcuff. Sure, the bracelet came with the sweater, and the sweater is what he bid on, not the bracelet. But I am unsettled. Something inside of me has come undone.

Remembering my manners, I smile. "Thank you." I open my arms.

He turns away.

I encircle his shoulders and kiss his smoothly shaven cheek.

He steps back and shoves his hands into his pockets. "Will you wear the sweater tomorrow when I take you out to lunch?"

"Sure." Our lunch dates have become a weekly

event. I crumple the box against my chest. Will people think I look like a circus clown next to a cowboy?

After placing the boxed sweater into the trunk of my car, I follow him inside the bank. Sitting at my desk, I edit loan documents. Every now and then, I glance at the black bracelet, the heavy metal coiled against my skin. Why did he bid on this outfit for me? He has two teenage daughters. He could have bid on something for them. Unable to focus, I set aside the documents and stalk into his office. I shut the door and draw the blinds. Spinning around, I gaze into his startled face. I sink into the chair before his desk and cross my legs. "How do you feel about me?"

He averts his gaze. "I—am—attracted—to you." He opens his arms wide. "But I'm just an ordinary guy. I think beer and chicken wings are major food groups. I don't have any passions, ambitions, or goals like you do."

I stare at his flustered expression. I unfold my legs and lean back against the hard chair. I think about you and the Empress. "I can have a boyfriend."

He finally meets my gaze.

The third denial is complete.

But unlike Peter, I do not instantly fill with guilt and remorse. Instead, I feel a gush of energy and focus. I straighten my spine and smooth my hands against my skirt. The heavy bracelet catches on the hem. I tug it free and wrap my fingers around the cold metal. "My husband is leaving to visit his girlfriend next month. I'm taking my vacation to be with the kids. I can see you then."

He taps his finger against the calendar on his desk. "What week is that?"

I tell him.

"I can ask for Friday off, and we can go to the beach." He smiles. "We can walk barefoot on the sand."

I have deceived you.

I do not know if you have deceived me.

But the deception clouds us.

~

THE NEXT CARD IN THE CELTIC CROSS READING REFERS to my hopes and my fears. What do I hope for when I ask, "Can this marriage be saved?" What do I fear if the answer is yes or no? I draw the Three of Swords. I stare at the image on the card of a blood red heart pierced by three swords in the middle of a rain storm. According to Sarah Graham, author of Llewellyn's Complete Book of the Rider-Waite-Smith Tarot, *the surgical perfection of the damage suggests the heartbreak is intentional, which makes it even more painful. Usually, this card is associated with romantic troubles, from love triangles to betrayal.*

Am I hopeful for the success of our two opposing love affairs—you and the Empress, me and the Knight of Cups? Or am I fearful my heart will break—or yours?

~

I NEVER TOLD YOU ABOUT THE CONDOM I FOUND IN your underwear drawer a week after discovering the unsigned greeting card in your vehicle. The gold packet gleamed between your balled-up running socks and your neatly folded cotton boxer briefs. I poked two holes into the foil packet with a sewing needle, hoping you would know of my findings without a confrontation and would walk away from your next encounter or, at least, be derailed by a trip to the gas station or any twenty-four hour convenience store.

By then, I knew the identity of the woman, where she worked, where she lived, what business you had with her. But I was powerless to stop you. The following week, as if to spite me, a box of twelve condoms showed up in your underwear drawer with a few stowed in the glove compartment of your vehicle. I wouldn't have been surprised to find one or two tucked between the dollar bills in your wallet. After all, you are the Magician. No obstacle is too great for you.

Years have passed since that uncovering. I know the woman is no longer a danger to our relationship—she has remarried and relocated out of the area. Your interactions with her have been reduced to an occasional email.

But a new threat bobs to the surface.

That woman, the Empress, you pined for that night you came over to my boyfriend's house and gave me the homemade chocolate rose, which I now suspect was originally intended for her and not me, has swum across the years to embrace you. She is expecting to spend a week with you as your guest at the business conference in Phoenix, Arizona. At night, you will travel to her home in Tempe where you will interact as the family friend with her husband and children. In the hours after her husband leaves for work and her children are shuttled off to school, the two of you will embark on your own adventures, either in the hotel's conference room listening to experts discuss marketing strategies to build your computer business or someplace else doing things I can't even imagine.

Since that period, years ago, when I found that errant condom in your underwear drawer, you've learned a few new tricks. You pack your suitcase strategically. Every item of clothing is rolled and stuffed according to an elaborate plan. If one item is removed, the entire configuration collapses. I cannot search the contents of your suitcase for condoms without being caught.

I ask Princess Pea if she knows how to undo what you have done. She is your protégé, a little mini-me, intuitive and calculating and confident. With one sweeping glance, she knows. "Mama, don't touch anything. It's a trap. You don't want to be caught."

Luckily, she doesn't know the real reason why I have asked for her assistance. She thinks I want to tuck a love note between your clothes so you'll discover the surprise halfway through your trip. She thinks I want to be clever and never have you suspect anything. She thinks I am a loving, trusting wife.

Unfortunately, I am none of those things.

I am selfish. I want to keep you here, with me, not there, with her. I want to spend my vacation hours with you at the beach or in the woods while the children are in school. We can stroll, hand in hand, through the Schulz Museum or watch a matinee after brunch at our favorite creek side restaurant that serves the best home-made biscuits and freshly squeezed orange juice. Or we can come back to bed and feed each other strawberries dipped in chocolate and lick whipped cream off each other's faces. We can luxuriate in our love, washing away the years of debris in our remodeled master bathroom shower. We can rediscover the magic of our marriage.

But, alas, I am a Fool. I think I can outsmart destiny.

You, on the other hand, are a Magician. You are my only hope of altering the future.

A week before your trip, I tug on your shirt-sleeve. "Please, don't go. We can spend my vacation together, just the two of us, while the kids are in school. We don't even have to come home early. We have the sitter all week. We can sneak in after the kids are in bed." I smile. "Like a second honeymoon."

You wince. "We never had a honeymoon, remember? We stayed one night in a hotel in Tiburon only because my parents took over our apartment."

I tighten my grip on the cotton material. "Then let this be the honeymoon we never had."

You toss back your head and laugh. "I can't cancel my trip. I'll lose my five hundred dollar deposit."

Is five hundred dollars the cost of our marriage?

I nudge you onto the black leather sofa, straddle your hips, and nibble your ear. "Wave your magic wand," I whisper. "Make the penalty go away."

"I can't." You wriggle out of my embrace and smooth your shirt.

Your hard look grazes my face. I gulp. You misspoke. You don't mean *I can't*. You mean *I won't*.

You spread your arms wide and gaze up at the ceiling.

I hold my breath, hoping you've changed your mind and will cast a spell.

"I need to learn the tricks of the trade so I can build my business bigger and better." You drop your arms to the sides and swipe your gaze across my body. "I've never stopped you from attending a writer's conference."

I shrink against the arm of the sofa. "No, of course, you haven't." I remember how my friend, Jan, paid for my entrance fee and hotel room so I could pitch my memoir at the San Francisco Writers' Conference several years ago. I didn't sell my memoir, but I did start writing contemporary romance. The initial draft of my debut novel, *Legs*, was scribbled on a yellow legal pad while I sat cross-legged on the queen-sized bed in the hotel room while Jan worked out in the hotel's gym. Why should I be selfish and keep you here with me? Why deny you the opportunity of a business breakthrough?

But we aren't talking about business.

At least, I am not.

Your words have cast a spell. Everything becomes illusion.

Standing, I take a step forward. "Then wave

your magic wand and make the Empress disappear." Exhaling, I clench my hands into fists. "You
did it once before, years ago, in the early days of
our marriage." I clutch my hands against my chest
in prayer. "Please, do it again."

You glance away and sigh.

I don't know if you're remembering that
moment when you traveled out of town to meet
her at a hotel. Once you arrived, she refused to let
you inside. The excuse—period cramps—as if a
little blood ever stopped you or anyone in the
mood for something more. Back and forth the
hurt and accusations flew through emails until
one night you strode into our bedroom and
announced the two of you were done—you'd
never contact each other again.

What sparked the renewed interest? I don't
remember. But isn't that the mystery of your
magic? What was once here is now gone. What
was once gone is now here again.

Finally, you speak. "I can't." You wrap your
arms around me and hold me close. "She is my
friend. I will not let her go."

Even though I am in your arms, I feel myself
float away.

The next day, at work, I stalk into the Knight
of Cups' office and plunk down into the chair
across from his desk. I am distraught with the
news of your imminent departure. I need
someone to confide in, someone who will take
away the hurt and the pain. I find solace in my
date with the Knight of Cups on Friday, but the
rest of the week yawns open. How can I fill the
hours of your absence? How can I stop fidgeting

with worry about where you are, what you are doing, and with whom?

Clasping my moist hands in my lap, I sigh. "I don't know how I can go a full week without seeing you."

He glances up from the email he is typing. "We don't have to wait until Friday to see each other. I can take you out to dinner earlier. Does Monday work?"

A date on Monday and a date on Friday would bookend my vacation. I smile. "Yes, I'd like that."

"Does six-thirty work for you?"

"Let me ask the sitter."

That night, I try to mirror the spell you have cast by cloaking everything in the illusion of work. I ask the sitter if she can stay late next Monday because I have a co-worker picking me up for a business dinner. We should be home no later than eight-thirty.

She consults with her boyfriend before committing to the extra time.

Next, I tell you about the business dinner with the Knight of Cups.

You do not object. Why would you? You are captured in the spell you cast.

We are both subject to the same terms and conditions. What is hidden from me remains hidden from you. The mirror of deception multiples the lies until we both don't know what is real and what is an illusion.

≈

On Sunday morning, I pack Forever Child and Princess Pea into the backseat of my sedan and drive you to the Schulz Airport. Your flight is so early the morning fog blankets the streets like a thick sheet of mist. In the loading zone, I get out and hug you goodbye. You smell of my favorite cologne, the one I bought you, all mandarin oranges, almonds, and cedar. You dip your head into the backseat and let the children wrap their arms around your neck and kiss you goodbye. The weight of your body strolling through the sliding glass doors leaves me.

As I pull out of the lot, I feel free for the first time in years.

That night, after the children are in bed, I stand before my closet and call my best friend, Scott. As an actor and a model, he is obsessed with fashion. When it comes to clothes, I trust his judgment.

"A coworker is taking me to dinner tomorrow night." I slide the hangers across the rack and remove three dresses and lay them on the queen-sized bed. "Which outfit should I wear—my black cocktail dress, my red dress suit, or my black and white floral ribbed dress?"

He huffs. "Why do you care what you wear to dinner with a co-worker?"

"Because…" I turn back to the closet and drag the hangers across the rack, searching for more options. "It's an expensive restaurant."

"How expensive?" Before the dot-com bust, Scott was a millionaire. Now he lives on a shoe-string budget, always rooting around for thrift shop deals. He complains if a dinner date costs more than sixty dollars, which consists of an entrée and one cocktail per person. "Where are you guys going?"

"La Gare." I roll the word off my tongue. For years, I've heard nothing but good things about the locally famous French restaurant, but I have never set foot inside the brick façade in downtown Railroad Square.

He sucks in his breath. "Work is paying?"

Heat flames my face. I can't lie to Scott, can I? After all, I've known him for thirteen years. I sold him his house. Our families know each other. He's attended our children's birthday parties. We confide in each other like siblings. But a lie spills out of my mouth just the same. "A guy I work for is paying as a thank you for helping him out while his mother was in the hospital." I study the dresses on the mattress. Red is the color of happiness, according to the Chinese, but the suit is usually my go-to power outfit for work. The black cocktail dress I typically reserve for date nights with you. By default, that leaves the black and white floral ribbed dress. "Never mind. You're right. I shouldn't worry about my outfit. I'll just wear my normal work clothes. I don't need help, after all." The words burn my tongue. "We'll talk later this week. Okay? Bye." I end the call, feeling like I've already said too much.

～

THE BELGIAN PSYCHOLOGIST ESTHER PEREL SAID infidelity is a search for the self, specifically other versions of ourselves which we are not currently living. Take, for example, the housewife of an accountant who spends her days shuttling children to school and hosting dinner parties at night. She might embark on an affair with a tattooed mechanic who rides a motorcycle and plays pool in dive bars. Perel would say the housewife may indeed be in love with her accountant husband, may even adore her children and appreciate the upper middle class lifestyle, but some part of her seeks to live out an alternate life as a woman unfettered by social obligations and familial responsibilities. In her lover, she can escape into a fantasy world as a rebellious young woman free to play pool for cheap beer and ride through the night on the back of a motorcycle with the wind playing through her long hair. Through the affair, she discovers a different aspect of herself, and that is why she clings to the lover and her husband— both half lives equal one whole.

I wonder what your alternative life is with the Empress. Are you a single, successful entrepreneur? Are you unencumbered and free? Who are you with her? Why can't you be that person with me?

On Monday, you text me with your schedule and send pictures of the hotel and conference room. You regale me with anecdotes from the speakers.

I ask about the Empress.

Yes, she is with you. She is learning how to expand her craft business.

I bite my lower lip, refusing to respond. What you don't know can't hurt you.

That evening, I slip into the white ribbed dress with the black flowers. The material hugs my curves. The evening is warm for the end of March, but I am always cold inside restaurants, so I slip into a black jacket.

At six-thirty, the Knight of Cups parks his truck beside the driveway. He strides up to the front door, and my heart leaps into my throat. My palms sweat, and I beam with excitement as I open the door and introduce him to the sitter, my Forever Child, and my darling Princess Pea.

After the brief round of introductions, the Knight of Cups and I leave, walking side by side, to the pickup truck.

Who am I trying to be?

Who do I want to become?

What version of myself is this stranger allowing me to explore?

None of these questions surface as I sit on the bench seat hugging my purse to my chest. "How was your day?" It is the same question I ask you when you come home.

He drives out of the cul-de-sac. His gaze is focused on the children playing on the street, the same children who move to the sidewalk as soon as the truck approaches. He swallows, and his jaw tenses. "Work isn't the same without you."

I sink back against the chair and gaze out the window.

He drives through the clot of commute traffic, past the abandoned warehouse on the corner of College and Cleveland, past the antique store with the rolling garage door and the old man who sits on the rocking chair smoking a pipe while waiting for customers, past the yoga studio and Redwood Gospel Mission where the homeless line up for the evening meal, and past Hotel La Rose and Aroma Roasters. Turning into the parking lot, he slides into a shady spot beneath an old oak tree across from the abandoned railroad tracks. Dinner reservations at La Gare are for seven. With a half hour to spare, he hooks his arm through mine and heads over to Chevy's bar for a drink.

Paper streamers dangle from mirrors behind the bar full of colorful bottles of liquor. The rise and fall of chatter intermingles with strumming guitars and trilling vocals pumped in through the speakers on the ceiling. Cool air gusts through the open windows, and the streamers flutter like long hair. There is magic and music everywhere.

I take a seat on a bar stool next to the Knight of Cups.

He orders two margaritas, one for each of us.

I have not told him I am a recovering alcoholic.

If I don't say anything, does that mean I want to become a woman who drinks again? Or a woman who doesn't need to worry about whether or not she will embarrass herself by saying something stupid or tripping on her heels or pawing at her date's shirt and pants like a starved and horny maniac?

I don't know.

I sip the tart and sugary drink, feeling a heady rush.

"Why are you taking so long?" He nods at my half-finished margarita after he has already ordered and finished a second one.

Stirring a straw through the cold slush, I shrug. "I don't drink much."

Why don't I tell him I don't drink at all?

I am creating a persona, a woman who drinks, but who doesn't drink much.

Fifteen minutes later, I slip off the bar stool and wobble on my heels.

"Careful." He places a hand on the small of my back and negotiates the distance from the parking lot to the front door of the small, dark, intimate restaurant. The owner, Jacquie, greets him. They have known each other since they were teens when the restaurant first opened. He introduces me, and I wonder how many other women he has introduced to Jacquie over the years.

We sit at a quiet table for two. Royal blue napkins sprout beside heavy silverware and beautiful glassware on the white linen tablecloth. A tea light flickers beside a tiny green plant. Paintings of the Swiss Alps decorate the wood paneled walls. A few stained glass windows featuring blue and purple morning glories allow the evening light to pool against the carpeted floor. The strains of a guitar playing a popular tune float through invisible speakers.

When I strip out of the jacket and excuse myself to use the restroom, I notice how his gaze grazes my body. I shiver with pleasure. Oh, how long has it been since another man looked at me with lust?

When I return to the table, I ask him about his past. He tells me about the future he imagines for us. Lots of trips to places I have never been but have wanted to go—riverboat cruises through Europe, snorkeling in Hawaii, fishing in Alaska. Lulls of silence fill the space between us. We are negotiating a new balance in our relationship, moving from co-workers to friends to lovers.

Who am I seeking to become in this transformation?

Who will the Knight of Cups allow me to be?

Why can't I be this person with you?

I tell him the same things I tell everyone else about me: I am an author and an artist and a wife and a mother. I ask him about himself and he does the same: he is a loan officer, a son, a father, and a softball player.

"When can I meet your mother?" I place the royal blue napkin in my lap and lean closer to the table.

He lifts his eyebrows, reconsidering. "You want to meet her?"

I nod. "You talk about her all the time."

After bowing his head, he scans the menu. "What are you ordering?"

I flutter my eyelashes. "What do you suggest?"

"The New York steak is good, but that's a big serving." He folds the menu and places it on the table. "I think you should order the chicken or the duck."

His comment bristles up my back and tightens across my shoulders. Why does he want to order for me? Why won't he let me choose what I want to eat?

With a sweeping glance around the warm, intimate room full of diners dressed in suits and dresses, I suddenly long for the simplicity of a meal with you, sitting on the plastic chair on the concrete patio of our backyard while you barbecue chicken or grill fish or smoke fresh vegetables drizzled with olive oil and garlic folded in aluminum foil. I dip my hand into my purse, glance at the screen vacant of messages, and wonder if I should interrupt your networking mixer with a quick text.

—*How was your day? Mine was okay. I started a new painting. A seascape. The kids are with the sitter. I'm having dinner with the Knight of Cups but thinking of you. XOXO. Hope your evening is going well. Say hello to the Empress and her family for me.*—

I don't type anything. Why should I ruin the illusion? As long as I am here, why not pretend I am someone else, someone important and glamorous, someone single and sexy? Why dwell on being someone who worries about what her husband might be doing 440 miles away? I tuck the phone into my purse and order the special —salmon.

With dinner, he orders a bottle of wine. But I am already tipsy from the margarita and can't finish a glass of red. He drinks the rest of the bottle with his steak and potatoes while I nibble on the fish, asking for a takeout box when I cannot eat more than a few forkfuls after the lentil soup, garden salad, shrimp cocktail, and flakey, crab cake appetizers. I notice when we leave that he is still walking straight and talking with clarity after drinking two margaritas and almost a bottle of wine. I, on the other hand, stumble on the sidewalk. He wraps his arm around my waist to steady me. After one stroll around the block, he drives me home.

But I don't want to go. I clutch the purse in my lap. How can I extend the evening? How can I prolong the illusion? How can I make the magic carry us over into tomorrow where I will wake up someone else in someone else's bedroom living someone else's life?

How do I escape being me?

After all, he is not you. He does not turn on the radio. He does not speed up to make it through the yellow light. He does not engage in conversation.

As he drives, he reaches over and works my fingers away from the strap of my purse. He curls his warm hand around my cool fingers and squeezes until the blood from his body seeps into my soul.

I am grounded, here, in the moving vehicle.

I am the beloved.

I am whoever he wants me to be.

I am reborn.

At the corner of our street, he releases my hand and places his on the steering wheel.

The absence of his fingers leaves me cold and dry and concerned.

I am no longer a single, sexy woman on a date with a single, sexy man.

I am a wife and a mother.

He walks me up the driveway to the front door.

"Do you want to come inside?" I wave my keys.

He meets my gaze. "No, you're tired. Let's say goodnight. I'll see you on Friday." He bends and places a closed mouth kiss on my lips.

The next day, Scott calls about the work date. He quizzes me like a big brother checking up on an errant sister. "So, what did you wear last night?"

The children are at school, and I am home alone. I tuck the phone between my ear and the crook of my neck. I am in the kitchen painting a seascape. I stand back from the canvas to see if I've correctly captured the light from the sky on the waves. "My white ribbed dress with the black flowers."

He grumbles. "That's *not* a work dress. That's a *date* dress."

When I refuse to answer any more of his questions, he drives over to inspect me.

I open the front door before he can use his spare key.

Anticipating a long, drawn out conversation, I return to the kitchen and wrap my palette full of acrylic paint in plastic wrap and place it in the refrigerator for later. I gather my dirty brushes and rinse the bristles in warm, soapy water beneath the faucet.

Scott paces the length of the galley kitchen, his hands on his hips. "Did he kiss you?"

My silence implicates me.

He places his hands on my shoulders and spins me around.

I gasp, dropping the brushes on the linoleum.

His blue eyes flash a warning. "Don't tell me you're dating this guy."

I swallow a hard lump of regret. I should have never called to ask his advice on what to wear. "I'm not dating this guy," I lie.

With a sharp inhale, he steps back and throws open his arms. "Why are you determined to ruin your life?"

I stoop to pick up my wet paint brushes. "It

was one dinner." I fill a cup and dump the paint-brushes to soak. "My husband is in Arizona having dinner with another woman. Why can't I have dinner with another man?"

"That man isn't just any man." He bundles his hands into fists. "He's not a friend of the family. He doesn't care about you or your husband or your kids. He's out to destroy your life." He swivels, eyes wide. "I don't want to lose my adoptive family."

His voice is thick with panic.

After drying my hands on a dish towel, I wrap my arms around his back and tug him close. "You won't lose us."

Gulping, he pulls away. Tears glass over his eyes. "Divorce changes everything."

I drop my arms to the sides and gasp. "Who says I'm getting a divorce?"

He sucks in a breath and holds it. Shaking his head, he releases the air from his lungs and leaves. The front door clicks shut. The lock turns. A car engine rattles to life and drifts away.

Alone, I sit on the couch in the living room. The house is quiet except for the ticking clock against the wall. In my lap, I fold my hands in prayer.

I want to be that woman who is married to the accountant but dating the mechanic, the woman who shuttles the kids to school and serves dinner parties. While everyone is asleep, she escapes from the house and climbs on the back of her lover's motorcycle. She wraps her arms around his waist and holds on tight, as the wind blows through her hair. At the dive bar, she drinks beer and plays pool, not as a wife and a mother, but as someone else.

I want my marriage and my family.

I also want the Knight of Cups.

~

THE THREE OF SWORDS IS A CARD THAT REPRESENTS our pain. But this card also appears to warn us when we may be inflicting cruelty upon others. When paired with the Magician, this card assures us we are not passive victims.

~

DURING THE WEEK OF YOUR ABSENCE, YOU CALL A few times. You ask about our children. You ask about my art. You ask about me.

I tell you the children are doing well. My painting of a seascape is almost finished. I am happy but I miss you.

Do you miss me, too?

There is static on the line, and a female voice calling. Where are you? In the halls outside the conference room? At a restaurant? At her house with her family? In your hotel room standing by the window with a towel wrapped around your waist while she lies naked on the bed behind you?

My imagination won't let me think neutral thoughts.

My imagination won't let me accept responsibility for my own actions.

My imagination won't let me live in peace.

When Friday arrives, after the children are

safely at school, I pack a few extra sandwiches for me and the Knight of Cups. I find the cooler in the garage and dump fistfuls of ice into the container and wedge a few bottles of water beside the sandwiches.

At 10 AM, the Knight of Cups arrives. I let him into the house. My easel is propped up in the corner of the living room. He strides over, hands on his waist, surveying the progress. "I like the color of the sky with the pinks and blues." He turns and smiles. "I like color. You should see my house someday. Every wall in my front room is a different color." He waves toward the painting. "I think you would like it."

I clasp my hands to my chest. When will I ever see his house?

The Knight of Cups transfers the sandwiches to the cooler he has packed in the backseat of his truck. He already has sodas and waters. "I never drink during the day," he says. "It makes me sleepy. But you're welcome to pack some beers for yourself."

Again, an opportunity to tell him the truth opens wide, but I skirt around the issue by not saying anything. I climb into the cab and shut the door and strap a seatbelt across my waist.

On the drive, he listens to eighties alternative rock on the stereo.

I remember how I confided in you about the Knight of Cups. "He won't open up to me."

"Ask him about what type of music he listens to," you suggested.

Now I am here, sitting in his truck, listening to his favorite songs at your advice.

You unwittingly are helping me seduce another man.

You are once again Cyrano de Bergerac.

The Knight of Cups is Roxane.

Why don't I think of us during high school? Why don't I see the parallels between then and now? Why am I so captivated by the alchemy of deception?

Other memories float to the surface. I've been to Bodega Bay plenty of times over the years. When Forever Child was little, after a morning stuffing flyers into mail boxes, writing advertisements for Sunday open houses, and processing real estate paperwork, I would drive to Doran Beach to escape hot afternoons in the stuffy apartment that felt more like a cinder block oven than a home. Before he could walk, I would cradle him in my arms and stroll along the moist sand, letting the cold waves lap at my bare feet. When he could walk, I would let him toddle wherever he wanted to go and I would follow him, laughing, taking pictures, and scooping him up into my arms before a big wave crashed over him. He would smile and giggle, his blond bangs covering his forehead. I nicknamed him, Surfer Boy, and dressed him up like a mascot for the Beach Boys. Sometimes people would join us, lounging on blankets, smearing sunscreen over our backs, nibbling on treats purchased from the ice cream and deli shop on the cliffs surrounding the beach. These moments are some of my favorite memories of being a twenty-something mother.

The Knight of Cups drives past Doran Beach.

He winds his way up to Salmon Creek and parks at the edge of a cliff.

I open the door, expecting a gust of chilly wind. But the air is still and warm.

He slings a backpack over one shoulder, gathers the cooler with one hand, and takes my hand in the other.

His grip is firm and comforting.

I follow him down a steep trail, careful to wedge my footing against the craggy rocks, until the soles of my sneakers melt into the gray sand.

He takes off his shoes.

I take off my shoes.

The act of mimicry plunges me into the depths of losing myself. I am no longer your wife or the mother of your children. I am him, the Knight of Cups. Scientists believe imitation happens reflexively with the beloved as part of the falling in love process. Cognitive scientists Lara Maister and Manos Tsakiris at the University of London studied 19 people and their interactions with both a romantic partner of at least six months and a platonic friend of the same gender as their partner. The researchers found that couples are far more likely to automatically mimic one another's movements, platonic friends, less so. This habit of mirroring the beloved is the alchemy, the mystery, the magic of blending yourself with your partner. Hence, the saying, two become one in marriage.

On the spring day on North Salmon Creek Beach, you are not here for me to imitate. You are over 400 miles away, imitating someone else.

Does mirroring the actions of the Knight of Cups undo us?

Or have we come undone already?

Right now, I don't know, and I don't care. I'm only conscious of fine, gritty sand between my toes.

A few steps ahead, the Knight of Cups holds his shoes in one hand, the cooler in the other. The backpack swings against his shoulder. After finding a space away from the cliffs and the waves, he sets the backpack on a rock, spreads a checkered blanket, and sets the cooler on top to hold it down against the occasional sea breeze.

Taking my hand, we walk along the waterline. Our bare feet leave footprints in the squishy sand. Salty wind blows through our hair. We smile at each other and the ocean.

The experience is better than the text message he sent weeks ago.

I luxuriate in the smoothness of his palm. You hands are callused from playing the guitar and lifting weights. I smile at the way the wind ruffles his brown hair, a little longer than you wear yours and slightly lighter. I marvel at the closeness of his taller, leaner body that smells as organic as the salt and the sand.

After a while, we stroll back to the blanket and sit side by side to talk.

"I hate feet, but you have beautiful feet." He gazes at my toes. "They are perfectly proportioned. I love the red painted nails."

I shudder. Who likes feet? Especially my feet. They are difficult to fit for shoes. Once, as a child, I cried after a day of shoe shopping with my mother. Everything was too big, too small, too narrow, or too wide. I felt like the ugly stepsisters in Cinderella. Now, against his long, broad feet with their crooked toes, my dainty feet are beautiful. I smile, curling my toes. "The Chinese worked really hard to produce the best feet in girls," I say. "They bound them for centuries, so they are practically genetic by now. That's why my feet are so small. But I am also German, and that is why my feet are wide."

He runs his toes along the sole of a foot. "You also have the highest arches."

His scratchy nails tickle. I wiggle, and warmth from his toes travels up my calves and settles in my thighs. I broaden my smile. "That's for wearing heels."

"You don't wear heels anymore." He leans over and kisses me.

The kiss is only on the surface, not deep like I prefer. But his lips are soft and gentle.

"Don't you French kiss?" I ask.

He shakes his head. "I don't like it, but if you want to try it, you may."

I part his lips and slip my tongue into his mouth. His tongue is thick and cumbersome, filling my mouth, leaving no room for my tongue to dart and flicker and explore. No wonder he does not like French kissing. He does not know how to do it well.

Giving up, I lie on the blanket and close my eyes against the sun. Why am I here? If I want to become someone else, I could have chosen a better lover. At least, I could have selected someone who knows how to kiss. I cross an arm over my face, further blotting out the rays of the powerful sun.

Who am I trying to be? Why can't I be this person with you?

I don't bother glancing at my phone inside my purse next to the backpack on the rock. There is no cell reception. I couldn't text or call even if I wanted.

What would I have texted you?

What would I have said if I had called?

Instead of reaching out to you through the haze of this lingering spell, I listen to the Knight of Cups tell me about his longest relationship with ex-wife, the mother of his three children. He talks about how they attended the same high school but didn't date until after college when he befriended her twin brother who suggested the match up. They ended up together for fifteen years, ten of them married. After he witnessed his wife step out of her car in a sultry dress to meet her personal trainer for a romantic lunch from the view of his third floor corner office window, he filed for divorce.

I remember the water cooler conversation about inviting him to work out with you and me at a local gym during lunch. His staunch refusal made no sense at the time. Now everything falls into place. He doesn't want to go to the gym because the idea smacks of betrayal.

But aren't I betraying you by being here with him? I turn onto my stomach and let the sun beat against my back. Closing my eyes, I listen to the drone of the waves. I am a woman relaxing on a beach with a handsome man. I am free. I have no responsibilities. I am part of the landscape, as integral as the cawing of the seagulls or the deposit of kelp along the shore.

I could have come here alone.

Why did I come here with him?

Who am I?

What have I done?

I know the answers to these questions.

I didn't come here alone because I would have dwelled on you—who you were with, what you were doing, when you were doing it, where you were when it happened, how did it feel, and why couldn't you do it with me.

I came here with him so I would not think of you.

I am your wife, the mother of your children. I am also a woman who is employed outside of the home. I do not belong to you alone.

Furthermore, I have done nothing wrong, not really, unless you count that terrible kiss.

What is it you're saying? Jesus was betrayed by a kiss.

You are not Jesus. You will not die for our sins. You will not rescue us.

Or will you?

I can't tell anything anymore under the lingering remnants of your spell, the one you cast to make me forget, the one you wove around us, so neither one of us would remember.

But I do remember.

The Knight of Cups and I eat sandwiches and drink cold water. Minutes pass into hours. The sun travels west, dipping closer to the horizon.

We pack up our belongings and trek up the cliff to the truck. I need to be home in time to relieve the sitter, who has an evening class at the university, and prepare dinner. I am not a free woman without responsibilities. I am an actor pretending to be one on this particular day.

On the way back to town, we stop at Armstrong Woods for a hike for one last romantic adventure. Holding hands, we amble along the trails. Several memories surface, but two compete for attention—the first time I walked these woods with my first lover, and the time my daughter hiked the trails with her class and came down with a virus that triggered her Hashimoto's disease. The woods, once kind and familiar, became as dark and dangerous as a Grimm Brother's fairy tale. Now, with the Knight of Cups, walking hand in hand and stopping only for soft, closed-mouth kisses, the redwoods take on another hue—the glowing pink flush of new love.

In the amphitheater, we sit on the redwood logs carved into stadium seating. The air is warm and thick with dust. Sun and shadows dance on my skin like winking lights through the branches. I listen to the Knight of Cups' childhood stories growing up in Santa Rosa. How, as a five-year-old, he would hike to Spring Lake with his buddy and fish all afternoon. They never took any of the fish home for dinner, just released them back into the waters. The sport was to catch and release, not catch and cook. "I can't kill anything," he says. "Not even a spider."

On the way back to the parking lot, the reception returns and his phone pings with a message. He reads the text and lowers the phone. "The guys are meeting for happy hour drinks." He checks the time. "Can you stay a little bit longer? I would love for them to meet you."

I know how precious these last few hours have been, but I also know how impossible it is to ask the sitter to miss class, especially during midterm tests. "Next time," I say, believing there will be a next time.

He types a response to his friends and sends the text.

In the parking lot, he lowers the tailgate and perches on the edge, pulling me into the space between his legs. He is so tall that when he sits, he is eyelevel with me. He caresses my lips with his pursed mouth. "I wish I could take you home."

I toss back my head and laugh, wondering if he wants me for the night or forever.

Finally, before we settle in for the drive to my home, we embrace for a long moment. I listen to his heartbeat through his T-shirt and run my fingers over the rough hairs on his arms. "I can't imagine returning to the office next week as if none of this happened."

He pulls me away by the shoulders and smiles. "We can meet in the file room and share kisses. It's completely private. No security cameras."

The thought is intriguing. I wonder if he has done this same maneuver with other women he has worked with at other banks over the years since his divorce. But I don't ask. I don't want to know the answer. I want to believe, if only for this moment, that I am the first, the one and only woman who has experienced this wonder with him.

I may be the Fool, but I am not naïve. I am

forty-three years old, and I know better. Every ray of sunlight casts a shadow. During the drive back, I want to know the underbelly of this romance. "What is your darkness?" I ask.

He turns down the radio and thinks for a moment. "I sometimes smoke weed with the guys behind the dugout after a game. And I drink too much."

I nod, already suspecting the alcohol abuse. "I'm allergic to weed, so please do not smoke it around me."

"Seriously?" He grips the steering wheel tighter, flashing a sidelong glance. "I didn't know anyone could be allergic."

"Weed is a grass. I'm allergic to all grasses." I tell him the story about how I bought hemp lotion and rubbed it over my arms in the hopes of curing my dry skin. Within minutes, my arms flared up painful and orange. You rushed me to the emergency room, and the on-call doctor gave me an injection to stop the allergic reaction. "Stay away from marijuana and hemp and all other grass products," he said.

I wonder if this revelation is a deal-breaker.

But he nods. "I can do that. I don't smoke it that often."

I have yet to tell him about the nine months I spent drinking after my first lover broke up with me. How I felt I could not live without him, the grief was so strong. I am not ready to talk about him yet. Maybe I never will be. Even the memory hurts like the tender skin beneath a healing scab. I cannot think his name without a rush of memories cascading out of my mind and into my heart, paralyzing me. All I know is I would have died from alcohol poisoning if I had not accidentally become pregnant by you. For a painful two weeks, I debated whether to have the child or abort it. I decided to take a chance, have the child, and save my life by delivering another life into this world. I bore my daughter to get rid of the pain of losing my lover, unaware he would return one final time to see the child I had with you.

But that was years ago, fifteen to be exact. A lot has changed, hasn't it?

At my house, the Knight of Cups parks, dumps out the melted ice from the cooler onto the lawn beside the driveway, and returns the extra sandwiches to me.

I invite him inside to rinse the cooler.

The sitter watches him move with alacrity in the galley kitchen, but she does not say anything.

After he leaves, I write her a check.

She silently takes it, the unspoken questions left unanswered between us.

Forever Child is listening to music in his room and shuts the door when he sees me.

Princess Pea is sleeping, still needing rest in spite of her thyroid medication.

I will prepare dinner soon, but right now the light is perfect—clear, strong, evening light—my favorite light of day. I move my easel from the living room into the kitchen, squirt acrylic paint on a plastic palette, and wet my brushes in clean, cool water. With careful strokes, I complete the seascape. High above the water, I add a road and a fence weathered by wind, rain, and sun. On the railing, I paint a heart-shaped wreathe with tiny pink roses. At the time, I do not know I am creating a memorial to my marriage.

~

THE FINAL CARD IN THE CELTIC CROSS READING IS THE outcome or the answer to the question. I draw the Tower, another Major Arcana card, referencing a flash of insight, a shakeup, or a truthful revelation that shatters the foundation of all previous beliefs. The card shows an image like the Tower of Babel with a king and a peasant tumbling from the fire-burning windows. What was once found becomes lost. What was once lost becomes found.

I remember reading about an auction of Sylvia Plath's personal belongings in which the tarot cards she received on her twenty-fourth birthday from her husband, Ted Hughes, were found bright and new except for The Tower, which sat on top of the deck, browned by sunlight from a nearby window. Why didn't Plath replace that card in the confines of the deck? Why did she leave it upturned and displayed for anyone to see?

A thunderbolt like the one in the Tower card powers through my body. Plath must have asked the cards a question in a one card yes/no tarot reading. Typically, in a reading about love, the Tower card signifies a bad omen pointing toward a breakup, a separation, or a divorce.

Did Plath divine the future of her marriage?

I shudder, staring at the symbol of destruction. Have I?

~

ON SUNDAY NIGHT YOU RETURN. I PICK YOU UP AT the airport with the children in the backseat. The process is reversed from last Sunday, and everything is different now. At home, you step away from the computer to go to the bathroom, leaving your computer unattended. The online chat is open. My heartbeat thumps in my chest. The cursor blinks like a winking eye. I stand up from my computer where I have been writing since the children have been put to bed for the night. I scroll up and read the dialogue between you and the Empress. My gaze catches on a line.

—*I'm in the shower. You're soaping up my breasts.*—

Is this something that happened? Or is this a current fantasy? How am I to know?

Before I can read the rest of the conversation, I hear the toilet flush. The cursor stutters as I scroll back to the end of the conversation and slip into my chair. Taking a deep breath, I arrange my features so I appear as relaxed as a writer deep in the zone, and not an anxious wife who just uncovered evidence her husband might be cheating.

You stride back into the room and resume the conversation, your fingers tapping away at the keyboard.

This charade of a perfect marriage can no longer save us.

On Monday, the Knight of Cups sends an email one hour into the work day.

—*I need the Morse loan from the file room.*—

The Morse loan? As in our own Morse code? Smiling, I type my response.

—*I'll get it for you right now.*—

Standing, I tell my staff I will be back in a few minutes. "I have to get a file for a loan officer."

Casey glances over her shoulder and grunts. "Better you than me."

I hear her. Before the file room responsibilities were transferred to our department, I wore three inch heels in wild animal patterns, mostly leopard skin and zebra stripes with red roses on the toes. Now I wear plain black flats to climb the staircases and scoop up thick legal files into my tiny arms. Using my badge, I unlock the door and step inside the cool chamber full of moveable rows. I walk down one aisle, pretending to browse for a borrower name under M. When the door clicks open, I hold my breath and wait until I sense the Knight of Cups' presence beside me.

I turn toward him, and he pulls me into his arms and places a kiss on my painted lips.

Closing my eyes, I swoon just like the cover of a romance novel.

He lifts his face from mine and shimmies my hips closer. "You're addictive like a drug."

I deepen my smile and reach up on my toes to kiss him again.

"Will you come to my birthday party tomorrow night at Cattleman's? You can meet my family."

I do not tell him that is the same restaurant where we held our wedding reception. I do not tell him there are memories binding us.

That night I tell you about the invitation. I leave out what I don't want you to know—the dinner date and the first kiss, the picnic at the beach and the hand-in-hand walking through the woods, the make out sessions in the file room—just as you have neglected to inform me about the details of your relationship with the Empress.

We are both guilty and pleading innocent.

We are both caught up in our alternative lives.

We are both staunch and unwavering in our web of intricate lies.

Of course, you allow me to attend the Knight of Cups' birthday dinner. After all, I have been faithful for a handful of years.

You trust me.

But I am a Fool who does not deserve to be trusted.

On Tuesday night, I follow the Knight of Cups to his house on the other side of town. Over the years, I have driven past the street, idly wondering about his personal life, but never daring to explore further. Now, the first things I notice are the crepe myrtle-lined streets with their pink and lavender blossoms and the roses blooming in the front yard and the white railing on the porch. I gasp as soon as the glass and wood front door swings open. The great room walls are painted vibrant red and blue with a white ceiling and gleaming hardwood floors. This man has another side to him, one I never suspected from his business suits and crew-cut hair and tasteful jokes.

A white and gray dog jumps off the green leather sofa and lopes over to me, barking and wagging her tail.

"This is my baby, Sophie." He bends to stroke the dog's head and back, whispering reassurances about the strange woman entering their home.

He gives me a brief tour of the dining, kitchen,

living room. His mother has completed some mosaics of seas horses, vases, and geometric designs that hang on the colorful walls. Even one of his daughters has painted a picture, melting different shades of blue crayons onto a canvas to show a man standing beneath an umbrella in the rain. No wonder he has responded so well to my own artwork—his family is full of artists.

After feeding and walking the dog, he drives me to the restaurant. Inside the warm room with the blazing fireplace, we take a seat by the window. I meet his mother, a tiny woman with a cloud of dark hair and the same clear blue eyes he has. She takes one of my hands in both of hers and shakes it gently. When she was sick with pneumonia in the ICU, he visited her every day. I tried to help him as much as I could at work, taking some of his responsibilities so he could leave early and arrive late. He showed me pictures of her on his phone, taken in the hospital, and his eyes welled up with tears when he feared he might lose her. "I'm a mama's boy," he told me. "She's everything."

When his children arrive, three golden and willowy teens, I shake their hands. Stanley studies me with an intuitive look, and I know he sees more than he lets on knowing. Stella jabbers away, not really connecting, too interested in her own teenage life. Stephanie, the youngest, is the one I feel like I have to win over. She is closest to her father and more hesitant. I know she is a ballerina, so I ask about ballet. Her hazel eyes spark to life, and she tells me all about her passion, playing Clara, the lead role in the Nutcracker.

During dinner, the Knight of Cups sits beside me, his hand clasping my hand on my thigh. Every now and then, he looks over at me as if amazed I am still here with him. He orders a mai tai because he says it reminds him of Hawaii, a place he wants to take me someday.

I don't remember the rest of the meal, from what I ordered to how much I ate.

Later, after dinner, he drives me back to his house. We sit on the green leather sofa he has had since his divorce ten years ago and make out like teenagers. When he asks if we can have sex, I tell him I only have sex with people I love who love me back. He gazes at me for a moment before he says, "Let's wait."

Minutes later, he changes his mind. "I don't want to waste this moment." He scoops me into his arms and carries me to his bedroom across the house and tosses me onto his queen-sized bed. Soon, we are naked. He rubs the tip of his penis against the lips of my vagina. I ask him if he has any diseases, and he says, "No, I don't. And I'm fixed too. You won't get pregnant."

But as soon as he slips inside, he softens and falls out. After several tries, he rolls over, covers his face with his arm, and moans. "I've never before had this problem."

I do not worry about it. The body knows more than the mind will acknowledge. I figure his body loves me, and the moment is not right. The mind and the body must be in agreement before the man can continue.

But the heat of lust licks against my skin. I am burning with desire. Dressing, I leave.

At home, I tell you about the birthday party. The talk does nothing to extinguish the fire ignited in my blood. Finally, I grab your hand and tug you down the hallway to our bedroom. Burying myself in you, I extinguish the flames as soon as possible. You don't ask about my sudden passion, and I don't tell you. After making love, you return to the living room and your computer and I curl up beneath the covers, send a brief text to the Knight of Cups, and drift to sleep.

The next day at work, the Knight of Cups suggests I come over for dinner and spend the night. He suggests this coming Thursday. "You can tell your husband we have to get up early to attend a work conference in San Francisco. Staying over will save you a half hour since you won't have to commute to the meeting place for the carpool."

That night, after the children are asleep, I sit on the black ottoman beside your feet while you recline in the black leather armchair to work on your laptop beneath a pool of light. I stroke your leg and ask you if I can stay overnight at the Knight of Cups' house. We need to get up by 4 AM to car pool. I have asked this favor of you once before and you agreed, but the trip was with a female co-worker. This trip is with a male co-worker.

Without glancing up from your work, you ask, "He has kids, right?"

"Yes, three of them." I do not tell you they currently live with their mother.

You shrug. "Sure. Have fun. I'll feed the kids and get them to school."

I swallow, dazed and amazed by your nonchalant permission. Some part of me expected a fight or at least a little protest.

The day of the sleepover, the Knight of Cups calls me into his office. "Sit down," he says, motioning to the chair across from his desk.

Worried, I clasp my hands in my lap and lean forward. My skin is cold and moist. The rest of my body is rigid with fear. *Is he breaking up with me?*

"I have the sniffles, so I have an appointment with the doctor. If I'm contagious, I don't want you coming over tonight. We'll reschedule."

My heart knocks against my ribs. Heat tears through my arms and legs, scorching my skin. My hands spring apart. I am both relieved and incensed. My overnight bag is packed in the trunk of my car. I do not want to go home. If he is contagious, I will check into a hotel downtown, order room service, soak in the hot tub and watch TV until I fall asleep. I do not want to return defeated. I want to escape for one night. I want to pretend to be someone else.

After he leaves for his doctor's appointment, I try to work but I can't focus. Casey comes over to my desk and asks what's wrong. "Are you bummed out you have to attend that all day seminar in the city?"

I lie and tell her I have mixed feelings about leaving the staff for the day.

She smirks. "Don't worry about it. We'll behave."

I laugh.

When the Knight of Cups returns an hour later, he walks by my desk with thumbs up. "We're on."

Relief unwinds throughout my body. My overnight romantic getaway will manifest after all.

After work, I follow him to his house. I park my car on the street and grab my overnight bag. Inside, he leads me to the bedroom and says I can take either sink in the bathroom. I place my bag on the floor without making a decision and return to the great room where he is cooking.

Sophie, the terrier mix dog, jumps up while he mixes wet and dry dog food for her dinner. She is an agile dog, eager for food, and full of love. She buries her snout into the silver bowl and laps up the sides, making sure she eats every last morsel.

I curl up on the sofa and watch him stir fry chicken and vegetables. The thick scent of soy sauce fills the air.

We eat at his long black dining room table with the TV news playing in the background.

"I'm not used to having people over," he says. "I talk to the dog and never expect an answer back."

Smiling, I consider how different our worlds are. "I feed the children first so I can eat in peace."

When it is time to go to bed, I slip into my pajamas and brush my teeth. At his request, I take the side of the bed by the window. "I've always slept on the left side," he explains. "For all the years of my marriage and all the years thereafter, and I don't think I would be comfortable sleeping anyplace else."

I don't complain. At home, I also sleep on the right side of the bed. Why change things now?

He rolls over and takes me into his arms. Slowly, he kisses me.

Soon, we are naked, trying once again to

consummate our relationship. This time he is successful. When it is over, he lies on his back and stares up at the ceiling. "I have a girlfriend," he says, meaning me.

I ask him to tell me about the other women he has been with, and he tells stories about six other women who have captured his heart or his head or just ended up in his bed. "I'm lucky number seven," I say, propping my chin on his chest.

"No." He grasps my hand.

I frown and squeeze his fingers. "No, I'm not number seven or no, I'm not lucky."

He covers my mouth with kisses.

The things we omit from each other are similar to the things I omit at home.

If I could step back and see clearly, I would know this relationship is not any different than the one I have at home. The dynamics are the same. But, in this moment, I don't know I am trapped in a device of my own making. I am too thrilled by the possibility of being someone else— a single woman with a single man living a separate life from the one I created with you.

The next day, at the bank conference in San Francisco, we eat lunch with my boss and one of the Knight of Cups' colleagues, another Asian American woman who has a crush on him. She preens over him like a mother hen or an adoring mistress, ordering his diet soda, shaking out his napkin before placing it on his lap, and offering a sample of her veal piccata on the tines of her fork. They look like they should be a couple, but they are not. We are the couple, sitting silently next to each other, not touching and not talking. We have just spent the night together and made love for the first time.

When the bank conference is over, I return with the Knight of Cups to his house to retrieve my car.

"Don't go yet," he says. "Walk the dog with me. I need to talk to you."

A prickle of fear ripples up the backs of my legs, but I agree to wait. I send you a text to let you know what time to expect me, and I let him take my hand and walk to the park with Sophie on her leash. The sky is blue and full of light. The air is still. The scent of freshly mown grass settles beside our feet as we stroll along the gravel path with pebbles scrunching beneath our feet.

Beneath the shade of an oak tree, he dips his head. "I want all of you. If I have to share you with your husband, I only want to be friends."

I gulp and tighten my grip on his hand. "Friends?"

I think back to the luncheon where the other Asian American woman doted on him. They will be closer than I will ever be with him if I choose to remain married. But I can't just leave, can I? After all, affairs don't work that way. Affairs are about sex and romance and fantasy and escapism. Affairs do not end in love and commitment and long-term marriage.

But some part of me does not want to go back to the way things used to be. I can't imagine sitting at my desk and receiving an email from him about work instead of about how he likes the dress I am wearing. I can't imagine stepping into the file room without being pulled into his arms and drinking in his kiss. I can't imagine driving past his street without turning down road and parking in front of his house and ringing his doorbell and being welcomed into his home.

I can't imagine a life without a hint of color.

As we circle back to his house, I think desperately. Once inside, I pace, telling him about my jealousy over the other Asian American woman and how affairs are always better than relationships because they do not change your life or who you are but they make you feel wonderfully loved and special. He does not comprehend my point-of-view, and I cannot understand his need for exclusivity. Finally, I stand in the middle of the great room and clench my fists and tell him my one and only plan. "I will go home and ask my husband if he is happy in our marriage. If he says yes, I will accept your terms and conditions and never see you romantically again. If he says no, I will file for divorce and be yours forever."

The Knight of Cups grabs my shoulders, trying to shake some sense into me. "I don't want you making this big of a decision because of me."

"Who else would I make it for?" I glance around, searching for a line of men who don't exist.

"I don't want to be responsible for ending your marriage."

"Then you should have been content to have an affair."

He releases my shoulders and shakes his head, slowly from side to side. "I'm not built like that."

Finally, after one last kiss, I leave.

At home, I step into the living room and notice

you sitting on the black leather armchair, your legs propped on the ottoman, working on your laptop. The scene is familiar, one I have witnessed countless times before over the twenty-three years we have been married. One child has been bathed and clothed and ready for bed. The other is currently in the bath. You wave a hand toward the kitchen. "There are some leftovers you will have to heat up."

For a long moment, I consider asking you right then and there if you are happy. But I am not ready to hear your response.

Instead, I stroll into the kitchen and place a pan on the stove and remove the plastic containers out of the refrigerator. While I heat up leftover spaghetti and meatballs, I try to formulate what I want to say and how I want to say it.

You stride into the kitchen.

After turning down the burner, I glance up at you. "Are you happy in our marriage?"

You lower your gaze. "No, I am not."

The sadness in your voice echoes in the empty chambers of my heart. With a sharp intake of air, I exhale. "Let's divorce."

You lift your face, your eyes as round and wide as marbles.

I don't say anything else. I eat my heated up leftovers, rinse the dishes, and place them into the dishwasher. I stalk into the home office and turn on my computer and the printer. Online, I search for how to file for divorce in Sonoma County. I print out the forms and leave them on my desk for tomorrow. Next, I wander into our children's rooms and say prayers with them and kiss them goodnight. When I return to the living room, you frown and wave the blank forms. "What's this?"

"I thought I should release you from our marriage if you are unhappy."

"Can't we talk about it first?"

I sit down on the black leather sofa.

"You weren't home last night and you came home late today," you say. "I've been working and taking care of the kids and trying to be both parents to them. Of course, I'm not happy."

Nodding, I fold my hands in my lap. "When was the last time you were happy?"

You lower the pages and stare at the laminate flooring you installed in the house seven years ago as part of the ongoing home improvements we have made to the fixer upper we purchased fifteen years ago. The length of your pause is unsettling, and I imagine the layers of memories you are sifting through—the countless sleepless nights when Forever Child gets up to eat waffles, the yearlong battle to get a diagnosis for Princess Pea's mysterious aches and pains and sleepiness, the drought of money that has never left us no matter how many jobs either one of us works, the battle of wills, the cultural differences that leave me feeling less like a woman and more like a man because I work full-time instead of being a stay-at-home mom, the sexual differences that claw at the seams of our marriage, the void of emotion that opens up whenever we pull away into our separate worlds, the spoken and unspoken affairs, the stretches of faith and togetherness, the moun-tains of sorrow from the first abortion to the final miscarriage, the disappointments from job losses and terminated book deals, the constant nagging nothingness at the bottom of it all.

Finally, you lift your gaze. "I don't know."

Twenty-five years of togetherness—two dating, twenty-three married—unravel with those three words—*I don't know.*

The things we've said and haven't said disperse like fog, revealing the ugly undercarriage of our marriage.

The spell is broken.

We are getting a divorce.

TAROT READING 3

CAN WE STOP THIS DIVORCE?

The Dinette Reading
(A Tarot Spread from The Housewives' Tarot)

he Housewives' Tarot is a deck of cards I purchased online. The cards, reminiscent of Anne Taintor's vintage images paired with modern sayings, mimic life's challenges as illustrated from the point-of-view of a 1950's housewife. The Minor Arcana cards are represented by common household items. The Suit of Cups, full of emotions, spills over with cocktails.

The Suit of Swords, all words and mental challenges, is knives from the kitchen. The Suit of Pentacles, reflecting material matters of daily life, is dishes. The Suit of Wands, creativity and inventiveness and spiritual growth, is symbolized by brooms.

The Major Arcana cards are also represented by household items: the Magician is a washing machine salesman, promising a reduction in housecleaning hours, the Fool is a housewife running above the roofline with the contents spilling from an open purse, the Empress is an award-winning baker, and the Knight of Cups is a champagne-pouring young man on a date with a debutante.

The dinette reading, much like the Celtic Cross reading, is for complex situations. The first card indicates my present interpretation of the situation at hand, "Can we stop this divorce?" I draw the Five of Wands. On the card, a housewife swats two dusters at a blender, a toaster, and an iron. Three more dusters are pinned to the apron over her dress. She is overwhelmed with household tasks that attack her from all angles. How will she get all the housecleaning done?

But I am not reading about a housewife tackling her household chores. I am reading about our marriage. In a love reading, the Five of Wands typically hints at a competition between people rising from jealousy, greed, or envy. Based on our situation, each of us entangled with another, I can safely assume the battle is between us.

∽

AS SOON AS THE FIRST GRAY, WATERY LIGHT LEAKS through the curtains my mother sewed for us as a housewarming present fifteen years ago, I roll over and rub my eyes. You are lying beside me, snoring. Heat radiates from your white, freckled back.

Did I dream the events of last night? Or did we really say we are getting a divorce?

I can ask for clarification later. Right now, I need to wash and detail both cars.

By the time I finish vacuuming the interior of both vehicles, the sun has burst through the cloud cover and bathed the entire neighborhood in warm, lemony light. I put away the bucket and hang the soft, damp, lambskin shammy over a plastic chair in the front yard to dry. Inside, I pad into the kitchen and turn on the espresso machine you brought home as payment for your computer services from a client low on cash but rich in appliances. The stainless steel wonder whirs to life. I double check the time—9:30 AM—before pressing the button for a double latte.

Between sips of the dark, rich, creamy roast, I gather the materials needed to bake the Betty Crocker coffee cake I make every Saturday morning. In the comfort of the glowing kitchen, I beat the batter into a silky smoothness and pour it into the greased tin. In another bowl, I combine cinnamon, brown sugar, and cubes of hard butter. I mash up the mixture with fork tines until the ingredients crumble like sand between my fingers. I sprinkle this not-so-secret topping on the coffee cake before sliding the tin into the preheated oven and setting the timer for twenty-five minutes. I cannot alter recipes like my award-winning mother, but I can follow a recipe faithfully to produce a consistent product.

While I wait, I soap up a sponge and erase the evidence of flour, sugar, and spices. I cannot cook and clean simultaneously like you, but I can make the kitchen sparkle afterward.

Footsteps creak down the hallway. The muscles in my lower back tense. I grip the handle of my mug tighter. I expect to see the tall, lanky form of our son demanding food at this hour, but the person who lumbers into the kitchen is you.

With a swift glance, I confirm the time—10 AM.

"Did you sleep well?" I ask, backing up against the firm counter.

You glower, knotting your fists at your sides. You are wearing a tank top and shorts, your bare feet splayed against the linoleum. "How can I sleep when my wife wants a divorce?"

"I just—want you—to be happy." I trip and stumble over the words.

Grunting, you shake your head. "You should talk to someone before you proceed to destroy everything we've worked for over the past twenty-five years."

My mind spins. Who I can consult with on Saturday morning? My thoughts circle back to the Knight of Cups, the only one who understands this dilemma. I would not be standing in the kitchen confronting my husband about the state of our marriage if I was not involved with him.

Princess Pea bounds into the kitchen followed by her brother.

I grab my phone off the counter and unlock

the back door to the yard. "If you watch the children, I'll make a call to talk to someone."

You nod, turning toward our children.

I step outside and close the door. The air is warm with a hint of moisture. As I take a deep breath, the freshness cleanses my lungs. Scrolling through my contacts, I find the number and press autodial.

The phone rings and rings until it switches over to voicemail.

After a slow intake of air, I say, "Call me."

Inside, I set my phone on the counter and set the table for breakfast.

We eat as a family, with you and I at opposite ends of the table, our children facing each other. We have fought in front of the children before but we are silent now, the steam rising from our skins like heat off asphalt.

Finally, my phone rings.

I glance at you, my mouth full of cinnamon and sugar.

You nod toward the tinny ring that amplifies the terror in the room.

Rising, I scoop the phone off the counter and step into the backyard.

"Hey, Cinderella," the Knight of Cup says.

The nickname warms my heart. He gave it to me when I could not stay until midnight for a work function. He doesn't know the name carries a deeper meaning, spanning from my childhood. I feel a deep tenderness toward him. "Hey, Prince Charming," I say. "Do you have time to talk?"

"I just finished softball practice," he says. "Do you want to meet at the parking lot of the bank?"

"No, I don't." My jaw tenses. Are there surveillance cameras in the parking lot? Won't someone review them on Monday? I rake my fingers through my hair. Who cares if our romance is discovered? If I am leaving my husband to be with this man, shouldn't I want the whole world to know? Obviously, I don't want to pretend whatever we are doing is illicit even if it is.

Tensions inside the household escalate. Between a bickering fifteen-year-old girl and a tantruming twenty-year-old disabled adult, I step inside, ready to battle. My gaze cuts across the kitchen table where the fight has erupted. I narrow my eyes. Didn't you agree to handle the children? Why ask me to tackle the questions of our marriage with someone else when you can't manage our children inside the home? A knot tightens in my chest, and a flurry of past transgressions flip like a cartoon reel in my mind— you couldn't leave work to take care of the children so I could make a million dollar real estate sale, you couldn't go back to a corporate job and abandon your business so I had to find full-time employment. The anger, bitterness, and resentment sour in my mouth. I narrow my eyes and lower my voice. "I have the kids, but my husband wants me to talk about what happened last night."

The phone is silent for a while.

Finally, he sighs. "How about we meet at Starbucks? I can be there in ten minutes."

"Fine." I end the call and wave my hand across the length of the table. "I'm leaving to talk to someone, just as you asked. Do you have things under control, or do I need to stay?"

You lift your hand. "I'll put on music for Forever Child and Princess Pea can help me clear the table."

Normally, I relish the moments alone in my car with the windows rolled down and the stereo turned up to the latest popular tunes. But today the short drive is quiet and tense. At Starbucks, I find the Knight of Cups waiting in a booth with a hot chocolate for him and a coffee for me. I don't tell him I've already had my dose of caffeine for the day. I am just grateful to see him. I slide into the booth, cup my hands around the warm paper cup, and quickly recount the events of last night. "What should I do? My husband is unhappy, but he doesn't want a divorce."

He stares at me with his sad blue eyes. "I can't date you unless you're a free woman."

I stare into the black coffee and wonder how to get around that condition. "I don't want to live without you."

"We could be friends."

Those words don't sound like us. I have had other male friends, and none of them have been this flammable.

We drink our respective refreshments in silence.

Outside, he walks me to my car and kisses my coffee-stained lips.

Nothing has been decided.

At home, a hockey game is playing on the big screen TV.

I set my purse on the coffee table and tell you I spoke with the Knight of Cups.

You erupt in fury. "When I told you to talk to someone, I expected you to call Scott or a therapist or a priest, not your lover."

I don't want to talk to anyone else. Not yet.

You throw up your arms. "I don't believe how foolish you are." You snap off the TV, shove your laptop into your carrier, and storm out the door. "I'll be at the office—working."

I don't bother to stop you from leaving. I have betrayed you. I don't have any right to make any demands.

You gun the engine and peel out of the driveway, speeding down the cul-de-sac.

Princess Pea wanders into the living room. "Has Daddy gone to work?"

Nodding, I sink onto the sofa.

She sidles up to me, tucking her legs beneath her hips and pressing her head against my shoulder.

She smells warm and fresh like a loaf of homemade bread. I kiss her forehead.

"He was going to help me with my homework after the hockey game." Tears bristle against her lashes. "You shouldn't have made him mad." Her voice cracks. "Now I don't know when he'll be home."

"Why don't you go play with your friends instead? You can finish your homework with your father tomorrow."

After a shuddering sigh, she leaves.

The house is quiet except for the rumble of

drums and the wail of guitars from Forever Child's bedroom.

I rub my face with my hands.

Oh, what have I done?

~

OVER THE NEXT WEEK, THE PUSH AND PULL between the Knight of Cups and you grows more apparent and unavoidable. During the day, the Knight of Cups and I sneak away for kisses in the file room. At night, we send each other text messages. You and I are civil to each other. No one has filed for divorce. We sleep in the same bed and continue with our normal routine as if nothing has changed. But everything is different somehow.

Princess Pea and I still drive to school listening to pop tunes. We "Shake It Off" with Taylor Swift. She tells me to stop drumming my fingers on the steering wheel, a pet peeve she's had for years. One day, I tell her what I know in my heart could be true. "What if I end up with the Knight of Cups and your dad ends up with the Empress in Arizona? How would you feel?"

She thinks for a second before asking, "Does the Knight of Cups have kids?"

"One son and two daughters. They are all older than you."

Her eyes widen, and she claps her hands. "I've always wanted more older siblings."

But her blessing slowly becomes a curse the longer I am with the Knight of Cups and the further apart you and I grow.

Worse, our daughter knows about my affair.

And once you are privy to this information, you ask her to choose sides.

I don't want to think about what a mess our family has become. I just want to escape. I start drinking, sneaking wine coolers into the house after work on the days I don't see the Knight of Cups. On the nights I do, I drink with him at his house.

A month later, the Knight of Cups asks me to go on a date with him immediately after work. We stop by his mother's house first to talk and have cocktails, then head over to Cattleman's for dinner. The restaurant is crowded, so we sit at a high table in the bar beside the carved wooden statue of a cowboy and the shuttered swinging doors of the main dining room. The warm air is full of the scents of steak and potatoes and sugary cocktails. Two TVs above the bar play the Giants game. Our favorite couch beside the gas fireplace is taken by two couples drinking wine and eating twice baked potatoes. I hang my purse on the hook beneath the table and let my feet dangle. We are drinking margaritas, and the cold, slushy booze rushes to my head. I shouldn't be drinking, since I will be driving home soon. But I've stopped caring. I drink whenever the desire strikes—in the middle of work, late at night while I'm home, in the mornings when I'm the only one awake, and of course, whenever I'm with the Knight of Cups. I don't see it as a problem anymore, but a solution to the frayed edges of my double life.

While I am waiting for our entrees, I receive a text message from you.

—*Where are you?*—

I lower my phone and steady my voice. Nudging the Knight of Cups, I show him your question on the tiny screen. "What do I tell my husband?" All these years I've been the one at home, texting you this question. All these years I've been anxious, waiting for your response. There are several lies I could pull from my bag of tricks, but each of them is flimsy and worn. You would see through them. You would confront me. You would ask me to come home.

The Knight of Cups shrugs. He does not realize how distressed I am. "Just tell him the truth. You're with me for dinner. You'll be home in a couple of hours."

I obey him. But he is not you. His words don't cast a spell. As soon as I send the text, you call.

My pulse spikes and my hands tremble. Since the night we discussed the lack of happiness in our marriage, you stopped scheduling clients after 5 PM. You come home at the same time as I do and eat dinner with our children. On the surface, we appear to be a unified family. But an undercurrent of tension flows beneath our false smiles and shallow conversations. We are at war, and we are the only ones who know it. Tonight, I am tired of fighting. I decide not to answer your call. I turn off my phone and order another margarita.

By the time the Knight of Cups and I stumble into his house, we are tipsy. He rips off my clothes, and we make love. He tosses my legs over his shoulders and rides me hard until he comes. I lay beside him only for a few moments, dreading the confrontation when I get home. The room is dark, and shadows play against the walls. I reach over and clutch his hand. "I'm scared."

He curls his fingers over mine and stares at the ceiling. His profile is fuzzy in the faint light filtering in through the slats in the windows. "If he doesn't let you into the house, you can come here," he says. "I'll leave the door unlocked for you. If you get inside your home and you're safe, just send me a text."

When I drive back, I park in the driveway and sit in the car for an extra minute to compose my thoughts. The house is dark. The automatic porch light has been turned off. All those years when I was home alone with our children, upset because you weren't home by the time I settle into bed at 10 PM, I would turn off the porch light in protest. I glance at the time on the glow-in-the-dark arms of my watch—9 PM. Too early for you to have retired to bed since you tend to crawl under the covers after midnight. I go to the front door, fit my key into the lock, and push the door open just an inch before the top latch catches. A jolt of adrenaline spikes my blood. I have never locked you out of our home, no matter how angry I've been. I ring the doorbell, not caring if I wake the children.

You unlatch the door and toss out my red suitcase. "Don't come back." You close and bolt the door.

In the pale yellow streetlight pooling in our front yard, I think about returning to the Knight of Cups' house and spending the night. But thoughts race through my mind, one after the other. Who will drive Princess Pea to school? Who will pack Forever Child's lunch? Who will relieve the sitter?

You will.

I wrap my arms around my waist, feeling cold and alone on this spring night. Some part of me is not ready to release you or our family, no matter the claim the Knight of Cups has made on my heart. I knock on the door, hoping you're on the other side and can hear me. "Please, may I come inside? Let's talk."

A few long seconds pass before the bolt clicks and slides back and the door opens.

I wedge my foot inside before I lug the suitcase into the kitchen.

As soon as you close the door and flick on the light, I lurch toward you with hands clasped I prayer. "I was on a date with the Knight of Cups, but I don't want a divorce."

Heat radiates from your skin. You twist your mouth in disgust. "You're a selfish alcoholic." You curl your arms across your chest, holding anger inside. "Give me one reason why I should let you stay."

I sit at the kitchen table and stare at my hands. On my left is the wedding ring. You saved for three months to pay the deposit and countless more to pay it off. On my right hand is the silver art deco diamond anniversary ring to celebrate the first twenty years of marriage. You bought it when I purchased a new wedding ring for you when we thought we had lost your original one at the gym before it turned up on the front lawn when you were mowing. "I love you."

"But you are fucking with him."

I love him, too, I want to say, but keep my mouth shut. Telling you I am in love with you and another man is not the best thing to say if I want to be let back into our home. I twirl one ring then the other on my fingers. "I'm sorry."

You drop your head to your chest and sob. "I don't know what you want from me."

I kneel down and unzip the suitcase. Along with the standard toiletries and underwear, you have packed my favorite nightgown, my hair brush, my bath salts, and my favorite work outfit. I sink down beside the opened suitcase and marvel at how well you know me. How can I keep betraying you? How can I not let the Knight of Cups go?

"I'll break it off with him tomorrow." The statement sounds final, a satisfactory resolution to our marital drama. I stand and wheel the suitcase to our bedroom. That night I hold you as if I am holding onto my life. I feel the warmth of your skin, the firmness of your fuzzy chest, the comfort of your strong familiar scent of amber and wood. But beneath the resolve, a niggling sensation spreads like tiny spider webs weaving a strong, invisible foundation in my soul.

The next day I march into the Knight of Cups' office immediately and tell him I can no longer see him. "I'm not divorced. I belong to another man. If I wasn't married, things would be different."

He listens, nods. "I understand. You're a stronger person than I am."

Two days of not speaking and not texting and not meeting in the file room leave me in withdrawals. I languish at my desk, pining for a glimpse of his body when he walks down the hallway to the copy room, the break room, the restroom, or the chief credit officer's office.

Even my coworkers notice a difference. Casey stops by and touches my shoulder. "You seem depressed. What's wrong?"

As a manager, I am not supposed to confide in my staff about my personal problems. I'm supposed to call the Employee Assistance Program.

On my break, I stroll out into the parking lot and dial the number.

The receptionist connects me immediately with a crisis counselor.

The woman on the other end of the line is kind but firm. "You don't really know this other man," she says. "People aren't necessarily who they appear to be at work. Most of the time, they behave differently in private. My advice is to give your marriage another chance. Find a new job. Delete all traces of this other man from your life— the sooner the better."

I pace the strip of sidewalk, glancing up every now and then at the steel and glass building where I work. "But I love the other man."

"Love is relative," the crisis counselor says. "History is more important. Family loyalty is more important. Your disabled son and your teenage daughter are more important."

"What about me?" I touch my breastbone with a cold hand. "Aren't I important?"

She chuckles. "You're only forty-three. You're too young to be having a midlife crisis."

The phrase smacks of derision. Her judgment

batters through my defenses. How dare she dismiss my concerns for my own well-being? Doesn't she know I can't take care of anyone if I don't first take care of myself?

At home, I don't let on I've spoken to a professional about the state of my marriage. I pretend I am handling everything just fine. I cook dinner. I bathe our son. I help our daughter with her geometry homework. I make love to you. I pretend we are a happy family, and I am the master of this universe, not a pathetic satellite circling an illusion.

Three days later, during my lunch break, I sit at the concrete table outside the bank eating leftovers from last night's dinner. Northern California is experiencing a heat wave. Sunlight blasts through the fabric of my linen dress suit, but I don't care. The living hell inside of me scorches worse than the blistering sun. I plunge my hand into my purse and withdraw my phone and send a text to the Knight of Cups.

—*How will I live without you?*—

Minutes pass. The sun slants across my legs. Glancing around the parking lot, I search for his green pickup truck. I do not see him. Toward the end of my lunch break, I stand and stride toward the double glass doors. My phone pings. I swipe my finger across the screen and read his message.

—*Easy. You do it one day at a time.*—

I curl my hand around the phone and shove it into my purse. How dare he blow off my feelings with a platitude from Alcoholics Anonymous?

By the end of the week, I can't control my emotions. I send him an email. "I need to talk."

He suggests meeting at the burger joint where we had our Valentine's Day lunch. Immediately after work, I slide my vehicle beside his truck in the parking lot facing Highway 101. I step outside my vehicle and climb into his cab. In the enclosed safety, I confess. "I miss you. I miss your kisses in the file room. I don't want to be just co-workers anymore."

He shifts his body against the steering wheel. "You miss the file room?"

His voice is hollow, and for a long moment, I think I may have lost him. I start to cry, shaking uncontrollably, and I hyperventilate in an attempt to control myself. If these emotions aren't part of a midlife crisis or an addiction or true love, then what are they and why do they overwhelm all reason?

He wraps his arms around me the best he can with the gearshift between us.

I gulp. "I want you back, even if it means I get a divorce." I clutch his dress shirt, my tears moistening the fabric.

"Are you sure?" He rests his chin on the top of my head and strokes his hand the length of my back. "You can't go back after you file."

But I don't intend to file. I intend to see the Knight of Cups on the side for as long as I can and keep you unaware for as long as possible.

My plan almost works.

～

THE SECOND CARD IN THE DINETTE READING REFERS TO what is currently passing out of my life, what will

*become my immediate past. I draw the Five of Swords.
On the card, a blue dress pattern is front and center.
Five scissors weave around the edges. A woman's hand
pulls a blue thread through the loops of the scissors.
Between a lack of planning and the chaos between the
scissors and the thread, the card indicates a hassled
housewife is trying to do too much and, as a result, is
doomed to fail.*

*Traditionally, the Suit of Swords references mental
challenges, a struggle with logic and reason, or conflicts
born from miscommunication. More specifically, the
Five of Swords in a love reading refers to an unexpected
change, anxiety, or irritability, which makes fights
between couples almost inevitable.*

∾

SHORTLY AFTER I VOW TO RETAIN BOTH MEN IN MY
life, you find my cell phone and scroll through the
messages. I sit at the kitchen table feeding Forever
Child breakfast. I think back on the secret texts
dating back from January and relax into the back
of the hardwood chair, confident you will find
nothing incriminating.

But the daily chatting back and forth ignites
your anger. Shaking the phone in my face, you
yell, "You have a relationship! He'll want to take
you away. He's not like your last lover. He will not
return you. Do you want to go?"

The anger radiates from your pores. I gather
up the dishes, wash and dry Forever Child's face,
pack his lunch, tie his shoes, and help him board
the bus to school. When I come back into the
house, I find a note you left on the kitchen table

written in your tiny script, the blue pen marks cascading downward on the white sheet of typing paper.

I am depressed.

I can't keep food down.

I can't sleep.

I can't find a way to end this nightmare.

I want to end my life.

The breath catches in my throat, and I race around the house to find you.

Curled up in the tangled sheets of our bed, you sob.

When I touch your back, you pull away, tug the sheets closer, and grow smaller.

Princess Pea stands in the doorway of our bedroom, her backpack slung over one shoulder. "What's wrong with Dad? I heard him throwing up last night. Is he sick?"

My mind trips back to the suicide note on the kitchen table. I swallow, step away from the bed, and nudge her aside. "I'll take him to the doctor, okay? I'll make sure we find out what's wrong."

She widens her eyes and points to the man on the bed who looks as powerless as a child. "He's sick because of you."

Hot shame douses me, and I race down the hallway, snatch the note off the kitchen table, and fold it into a tiny square that fits inside the zippered compartment in my purse. "I need to drive you to school first."

She trails after me into the kitchen and tilts her head to the side. "I'm not leaving Daddy. He needs to come with us."

I glance at the clock. Ten minutes until the bell

rings. "You'll be late."

She narrows her gaze.

The sensation of falling plunges through me, and I lunge down the hallway and into the bedroom and shake your shoulder. "You're coming with us to drop off Princess Pea to school. Then I'm staying home and taking you to the hospital."

Footsteps patter down the hallway. I feel our daughter's gaze burrow into my back. *She knows.* Of course, she knows.

Somehow you find the strength to dress and slip into the backseat of my four-door sedan.

The drive is quiet, although I have turned on the radio and rolled down the window to let crisp, fresh spring air into the stuffy interior.

When I pull up to the horseshoe driveway and lean over for a goodbye kiss, she stares straight ahead, refusing to acknowledge me. She opens the door and leans her head into the backseat and kisses you goodbye. Her arms wrap around your neck and her long, brown hair falls over your face. She shudders for a moment, then draws away and runs. Taking the steps two at a time, she leaps up the staircase to the main entrance and disappears. Watching her leave, I feel the first shiver of reality bend the illusion I have been cherishing this whole time—if we divorce, I may never see her again, she may decide to live with you, she may not want to talk to me, she may disown me like you disowned your mother, years ago, after Forever Child was born. For three years, you returned her mail unopened, deleted her voice mails on the answering machine, and refused to attend any family functions because you suspected she was the person who called Child Protective Services on us when our son refused to reach all the typical milestones of rolling over, sitting, and crawling because she believed we held him too much. Only later, after he was diagnosed with so many disabilities we had to carry around a business card to hand to strangers who may not understand why he behaved the way he did, the hurt and betrayal slowly eased into love and forgiveness. But those three years will forever be lost.

How many years will I have to suffer to pay for the sins I've committed?

Instead of pulling out of the horseshoe driveway, I shift the car into Park and dial the bank. I ask the receptionist to transfer me to Human Resources. As soon as Pam's sturdy voice answers, I blurt out, "I need to take a day off. I have a family emergency."

"Will you be using your vacation hours or are you requesting family leave? You'll need a doctor's note for family leave."

I glance in the rearview mirror at your pale face turned toward the school's entrance. "I don't know how much time I'll need and I don't know if I can get a doctor's note. My husband is sick."

She sighs.

I hear tapping in the background like she is at her computer, typing on the keyboard, researching my options.

"You can use your sick time up to ten days. After that, you will either have to use your vacation hours or get a doctor's note for family leave. The bank's policy allows up to twelve weeks of paid family leave to care for your husband."

Twelve weeks is three months. In California, a divorce takes a minimum of six months.

But no one has filed for divorce. Maybe I am worrying about nothing.

I end the call and wave you to the front seat. "We're going to the beach."

You get out of the car and slump beside me.

I pull out of the horseshoe driveway and merge onto the main street.

We take the same roads I took with the Knight of Cups. But instead of driving further north to Salmon Creek Beach, I take the first left and wind down to Doran Beach. I used to take Forever Child here before his sister was born. I find a parking spot and open the door and step out into the blustery wind. The searing cold whips through my business suit dress. I kick off my shoes and shimmy out of my pantyhose. My bare feet are splayed against the blacktop.

You step outside, frowning, and tug a baseball cap over your eyes.

We walk to the nearest picnic table. The air is brisk and salty. The coarse, gray sand is cold and damp between my toes. I slide across the wooden bench facing the roiling waves of the ocean. We are alone except for the sea gulls diving into the white crests and a man jogging along the shoreline. I reach for your hand, but you tuck it into your pocket.

For a long while, no one speaks.

"You haven't stopped seeing him. You're just getting better at hiding it." You place your arms on the table and gaze at the ocean. You swallow and tears silently stream down your cheeks. "He says, 'I don't like being touched. Only by my kids. And now you.'"

You slay me with your venomous gaze.

"How do you touch him?"

The forcefulness of your words hits me like gale winds. I sway, almost tipping off the bench. What can I say? The truth will destroy us.

You remove the baseball cap and run your fingers through your thinning hair. "Why do you find him attractive? What does he have that I don't? A powerful position? A better house? Normal kids? Lots of money?"

The list of reasons marches across my mind. Nothing registers. "I like the way I feel when I am with him." A sensation tingles across my skin, suffusing me with unexpected warmth. "Everything I do and everything I am amazes him." I recall our conversations at the loan documentation counter beside my desk and the emails I've printed and saved from my work computer. "He thinks I'm beautiful and smart and talented. He wants to pay for me to go to the Book Expo in New York to promote my memoir. He believes I have a chance of being as big as Stephen King."

You scoff. "What does he know?" You narrow your gaze. "Does he read?"

I stiffen. "No, he doesn't."

"Then everything he says is hogwash."

Hogwash. I cringe. Have I been so caught up in the fantasy everything has transformed into one big delusion? The publisher has ordered 3,000 copies to be printed. She says the bookstores are preordering in unprecedented numbers. I've hired a publicist and scheduled a nationwide book tour in October. What if you are right and everyone else is wrong? *Hogwash.*

I scrub my eyes with my fists, fighting back tears.

"No one knows what goes on behind the scenes." You fold your hands on the table and lower your voice. "The early mornings writing, the late nights editing, the constant juggle between time and money, the years of sacrifice." You blink back tears and uncurl your hands. "More people watch TV and movies on streaming services than they read books. Sure, you have a good story. Yes, it's well written. But is it the same caliber as Stephen King? No, it's not. I've read everything he's written. His stories are well paced, full of psychological suspense and horror. He knows how to capture your attention and keep you turning pages even though his books rival the size of the Bible." You meet my gaze and shake your head. "You write small stories about everyday people encountering everyday problems. No one wants to read about that unless they are looking for a solution to their own lives and you can deliver that remedy. Your tale isn't self-help memoir. Your story is about a little girl who was treated poorly by her father who came from a different culture. How is that story going to help readers?"

I bow my head, letting your words sink into me like rain on dry grass. "I don't know."

"People read for two reasons—to be entertained or to be educated."

I think about the school in the Midwest whose teacher has assigned my book as required reading. All those students are hoping to be educated by my words. Tension knots across my shoulders. What will they learn?

"Your boyfriend doesn't know anything about you or the publishing industry. He's just some guy who likes your pretty face and the fact that you laugh at his pathetic jokes. He's not a good person. He can't be if he's determined to break up a happy family."

I shift on the bench, anger bristling up my back. "You said you weren't happy."

"No one is happy all the time."

"When was the last time you were happy with *me*?" I tap a thumb at my breastbone and heave a breath, waiting.

You return your gaze at the ocean and refuse to respond.

The network inside my body feels like tiny fissures radiating from my chest into my arms and legs. If I move too suddenly, the fissures might break and my internal structure will collapse. I don't know what to do, where to go, or how to get out of this thicket of trouble I've created.

And, glancing over at you with your forlorn gaze and defeated posture, I suddenly realize even your magic can't save us.

∾

AT HOME, YOU PROMISE NOT TO KILL YOURSELF. Instead, you move your belongings out of the master bedroom and into the office. You transfer my belongings into the master bedroom including my desk, my computer, my bookcase, and my doll collection.

Our daughter notices the changes when she arrives home from school. "What's happening?"

We are like two enemy countries staking territory in our house.

Neither one of us explains to our daughter what has shifted in our relationship. Maybe because neither one of us understands the divide we've created in order to work through our differences.

As the weeks progress, nothing changes. We co-parent the children like we always have, tag teaming the demands of the Forever Child, and negotiating the shifting needs of Princess Pea. I try my best to come home by six-thirty, carving out that one hour after work for the Knight of Cups. I tell him not to text me after work, especially not on the weekends, but he says it's too hard. He wants me with him all the time. He wants to introduce me to his friends, take me with him to his softball tournaments throughout Northern California and Nevada, and spend evenings with his mom enjoying cocktails and dinner and the sunset from the deck in her backyard. Even though the offer sounds enticing, I am struggling to keep my marriage together. I don't want a divorce, but I don't want to limit my freedom. I still want to be the perfect wife and the perfect girlfriend for two different men.

After a month of living a truce with you on the couch and me in the queen-sized bed, we crash into another dead end. I haven't stopped drinking or seeing the Knight of Cups. Sometimes I will order a beer during my lunch hour, stop at the liquor store, and down another pint of whatever cheap alcoholic drink I can find before arriving home. I've started blacking out, not remembering everything from the moment I step inside our living room to the moment I wake in the morning. You've started recording my drunk and angry soliloquies on your cell phone. I pound my fists against your chest, demanding you stop. You remind me you can call the police and file a domestic violence report if I keep touching you.

Each day our children witness us actively destroying whatever good there is left between us.

Finally, on one Saturday morning, our son wanders into the hall, all newborn calf legs. "Eat." He totters past us, unheeding the fight between us.

His basic demands—eat, sleep, bathe—diminish our ever expanding needs—love, unity, happiness, freedom.

You turn and leave to feed him.

I slip outside into the backyard and take a seat at the plastic picnic table. The morning sun has yet to crest over the roofline, and I shiver, tugging my sweatshirt close to my breasts. For once, I am sober. I have drunk two cups of espresso and eaten two slices of my homemade coffee cake.

The door cracks open and you step onto the concrete patio. You pull back a chair and sit next to me.

The anger between us has lowered to a simmer. Conflict creates tension, and tension needs to be released. But we don't even hold hands anymore. Every time I bring up your involvement with the Empress, you deny your relationship with her. "We're just *friends*," you say, as if the word absolves you from any responsibility.

Why should I shoulder the blame alone?

We don't have an open marriage, but we've always operated on a swinging door policy. No matter who strays, we always return. Why can't we keep up this routine?

"Wait for me." I meet your gaze.

Your jaw is set and firm. Your gaze fixed on some distant point I cannot see. "Not this time."

I heave a sigh, refusing to believe this statement is your final answer. Eventually, things will settle. The Knight of Cups will retire, move away, and start a new life with someone else. The Empress will grow bored of a long distance, once-a-year-relationship and find someone closer to home who she can see more frequently. At this juncture, I image we'll return to each other and rebuild our marriage one brick at a time like we've always done.

~

THE NEXT CARD IN THE DINETTE READING REVEALS MY immediate future. I select the Five of Pentacles. The card shows a housewife dropping five plates. The first one shatters on the floor. The Suit of Pentacles covers the material aspects of life, such as work, business, trade, property, and physical possessions, basically anything of monetary value in the world. Specifically, the Five of Pentacles refers to adversity, financial struggles, and insufficient resources.

~

THE RECEPTIONIST RINGS MY DESK.

"Yes?" I am not expecting any visitors—no client signings, no friends who might stop by to see if I'm available for lunch. All my time has been shifted to accommodate the Knight of Cups.

"Someone is here at the front desk to see you."

Who is this mystery person? I push back my chair, stand, and stride down the hallway past the cubicles of the loan operations department, the closed offices of the credit administration staff, and the open air offices of the accounting department.

A woman I have never met before extends her hand. "You have been served," the stranger says.

I clutch the sealed envelope in my limp hand.

The receptionist catches my eyes.

I drop my gaze and turn, shuffling back to my desk. With quivering fingers, I break the seal and withdraw the document drafted weeks ago but signed and delivered today. After tucking the petition and summons for dissolution into the envelope, I send an email to the Knight of Cups.

—*I was served divorce papers just now.*—

His response is immediate.

—*Well...what were you expecting?*—

Air deflates from my lungs. I turn off my monitor and stack the papers on my desk. *What was I expecting?* I sit back and think. Months have passed since the Knight of Cups and I have evolved from friends to lovers. Even though you said you would not stand by and wait for another affair to end, I never expected you to take the legal steps needed to end our union. After all, you said you didn't want a divorce. Why file if you don't want things to end?

My boss, who I have not told about my wild love affair, calls me into her office.

On shaking legs, I stand and wobble down the hallway and close the door.

She motions for me to take a seat. Her dark eyes gaze at me with a tenderness I feel is imagined. But once she folds her hands on the desk and leans forward, her concern is real. "If you need any help with the divorce process, please let me know."

I arch my eyebrows. "How do you know?"

She shrugs, but her gaze drifts toward the reception area.

I gulp. Who else knows?

As I walk back to my desk, I scan the cubicles, searching people's faces. Does the loan servicing manager know? Do the loan officers know?

I sink into my chair and turn on my monitor. The IT department knows. They read everything. I wonder why I haven't been called into Human Resources and reprimanded.

When I tell the Knight of Cups, he says the office policy does not prohibit personal relationships between individuals in different departments. We are exempt.

But I can't focus. All of my thoughts circle like vultures around the wreckage of my marriage. I type an email, erase it, and type it again, before deleting it. I don't want anyone else to know what a mess I've made of my life. I pick up the phone, dial the Knight of Cups' extension and hang up when the call goes to voicemail.

Standing, I leave the department. I travel past his office, two doors down from the file room. He is on the phone with a client. He sees me through the window and holds up his hand signaling five minutes.

I swipe my keycard and the file room door clicks open. I step into the cool, windowless, camera less room and find refuge in the aisles of loan files stacked in alphabetical order. The air smells like old books. It is almost as comforting as being in a library. A hush settles over me, and I stroll back and forth, waiting.

Finally, the door clicks open. Moments later, he strides up to me and folds me into his arms. "I'm sorry you're so upset." He lowers his mouth and kisses me.

The door clicks open again. "I know you're in there," a woman shouts.

The aisles start to compress inward like a trash compactor. I hit the stop bar with my foot, and he rushes out of the walls of files that have temporarily stopped moving. Bickering voices rise up like steam and disperse. The door clicks and feet stomp out. I wait until silence settles all around me, and I am alone.

What just happened?

I swallow the tension in my throat and leave the file room. The warmth of the office travels over the length of my body, and I am dripping in perspiration before I stalk past his office to my desk.

Within moments, the Asian American loan officer who attended the conference with us in San Francisco yanks the filing cabinet beside my desk and removes her loan documents and files. Her movements are sharp and precise.

"What's wrong?" I stand, alarmed by her

behavior.

She doesn't answer. Turning, she storms out of the department and slams the door to her office, which is right next to the Knight of Cups.

Casey, who has witnessed everything, perches on the edge of my desk. "She acts like a woman scorned."

Cold dread forms a headband of sweat against my forehead. *She was the one shouting in the file room.* She's angry. She's jealous. She wishes she was the one who won the Knight of Cups' heart.

Within minutes, I receive a call from Pam, the Human Resources manager. "I need to see you," she says.

I shudder. Standing, I smooth my skirt and grab a notebook and pen in the event I need to jot down whatever will be said. Nothing is going as planned, nothing at all.

But once I step into the office and close the door, Pam smiles and waves to the seat across from her. "This meeting is only a formality," she says. "There's been a complaint to upper management about inappropriate behavior in the file room that has created a hostile work environment."

I gasp. That Asian American loan officer told on us. She filed a grievance. Will I end up divorced *and* jobless? The weight of the pressure settles against my chest, and I lean back and close my eyes and struggle to breathe. Just breathe.

"Don't worry," Pam reassures me. "I can't fire you. There is nothing in the employee handbook that prohibits love affairs between individuals in different departments."

I open my eyes and nod. "That's what I thought."

She lowers her glasses and holds my gaze. "I would, however, cool it in the file room. Keep everything professional on site. Even our married co-workers don't hold hands during work hours."

I nod, understanding blossoming inside. No file room. No problem. "I'm getting a divorce. My husband just filed. I was served earlier today."

"I'm—sorry?" She stammers. "I mean, these things happen, but sometimes mistakes can be rectified—unless you *want* the divorce."

I shake my head. My shoulders slump forward, and I crumple a sheet from my notepad.

"I have time tomorrow." Her voice is soft and warm. "Would you like to grab lunch?"

The offer is an olive branch. "Yes, I would like that very much."

The next day, we meet at a Vietnamese restaurant. We order and sit at the bar alongside the back wall facing the parking lot.

"I was married once before," Pam says, pushing up her glasses. "We were high school sweethearts. We were happy. Then we were not. He filed. I didn't know what was wrong. I was depressed for years." She rips open a packet of sriracha and dumps it into her bowl of pho noodles. "I met my current husband while online gaming. He's from Canada. We traveled long distance for four years before I asked him to marry me."

I drop my chopsticks. "*You* asked him to marry you?"

She nods. "He wasn't motivated to move to the United States, and I was tired of international travel. My proposal was the push he needed to come here and be with me full time. We've been married twice as long as my first marriage."

She doesn't look that old—maybe forty or forty-five. But her gaze is gentle and compassionate.

"I'm here if you ever need a friend to talk to," she says.

As soon as Scott finds out the news, he invites me to lunch and interrogates me. "You said God talks to you. Sometimes the devil assumes God's persona to tempt you to do evil. Did you ever think the devil was asking you to leave your family?"

I sit back against the vinyl booth, holding the plastic menu in my dry hands. I never once considered the possibility of the devil masquerading as God. "Besides, I didn't file. My husband did."

"Remember my parents' divorce?" He narrows his gaze and stabs the straw in his glass of lemonade. "Whoever leaves the house loses the house. Whatever you do, don't leave."

But where will I go? The situation has become untenable. We can no longer live together.

"My friends rented an apartment and switched off every other week during their divorce so their kids could stay in the same home."

"What happened *after* the divorce?"

He averts his gaze and heaves a sigh. "He found a man's underwear in her dresser drawer and had a fit. She found a box of condoms in his night stand and cried. Eventually, they sold the house and bought two condos instead." He gulps and brushes a hand over his eyes. "I can't believe you're breaking up my adoptive family." Tears glisten against his cheeks. "You swore you would always work things out. That's why I stick around. My wife and I are too old to have children. Your children are *our* children. Your home is *our* home. How can you hurt *us*?"

I fold the menu and set it on the table. "None of my other affairs caused this much trouble."

He thumps his fist against the table. The glasses rattle, and liquid sloshes over the sides. "You shouldn't be having *any* affairs."

How can I argue? I agree. I should be faithful. I should be happy. I should be a good wife, a good mother, a good employee. I should, should, should….be, be, be…

But I'm not.

When I return to the bank, I have a voicemail from the IT department.

I flinch, recalling the emails, the voicemails, the phone calls, the cameras.

"I'll be right back," I tell Casey. "I'll review your docs after my meeting upstairs."

"Compliance?" She arches an eyebrow.

"IT."

She bites her lower lip and nods.

I haven't told her about my affair with the Knight of Cups, but by now I assume everyone knows.

I still haven't taken any steps to respond to the petition and summons. The Knight of Cups has made an appointment tomorrow for me with the attorney who represented him and his ex-wife during their divorce. We will take two vehicles, leaving ten minutes apart. We are still sneaking around like two errant teenagers, not two irresponsible adults.

After climbing the stairs and swiping my keycard next to the door, I enter the upstairs offices and round my way to the IT manager's office.

I slump in the chair, without bothering to close the door.

Chandran kicks the door shut and leans against the desk, crossing his arms over his chest. "I need your cell phone and the keys to your car."

Sitting up, I widen my eyes. "Why?"

"I know your husband. He's going to put up a fight. And you need a wizard on your side." He spreads his arms wide. "I am Wiz Dum on the dark web. Your husband is Lord Wrath. We are enemies, but we also know each other's tricks. He will use whatever he can to destroy you in the divorce."

I wipe my damp hands on my skirt. "Why didn't you alert HR as soon as you knew?"

He tosses back his head and chuckles. "Why? Your romance with the Knight of Cups is better than any Bollywood movie I've ever seen, and I've watched thousands of them." He points to the fingers on one hand. "Your productivity hasn't decreased. You haven't breached our privacy policy. You aren't posting on social media or shopping for shoes and clothes. Why stop a little romance?" He shifts his weight and stands. "I called you up here to protect you." He extends his arm, palm exposed.

I open my purse and withdraw my key ring and my cell phone.

Within minutes, he has changed the passwords and programmed the phone for two-step verification. In the parking lot, he slides beneath my car and reemerges empty-handed. "No GPS device." He shrugs.

"What do I owe you?" I squint at him in the sunlight.

He smiles as he holds open the glass door. "Don't have an affair with my wife." He laughs. "Seriously, I'm pleased to have outsmarted Lord Wrath."

That night, after dinner, you follow me to the master bedroom. You shut the door and ask to see my phone. I hand it over, my heartbeat pulsing against my skin.

You swipe your finger across the screen. Nothing. You tap at the keypad. Nothing. You toss the phone on the mattress. "Why did you change the settings on your phone?"

"I didn't."

"Who helped you?"

Your hot breath blisters my face. "No one." I lie.

"I don't trust you." You flare your nostrils and point to the door. "You need to move out."

Whoever leaves the house loses the house.

The next day, I arrive at the attorney's office in downtown Courthouse Square. The Knight of Cups arrives ten minutes later. Together we sit side by side in front of Mr. Tyreck, a blustery middle aged man with comb-over hair and a bulbous nose. He examines the tax returns I brought, the deed to the house, the mortgage payments, the various bank statements and credit card bills. I hold my breath, crossing and uncrossing my ankles, my fists knotted in the straps of my purse.

He huffs, waving to the fan of papers on his broad desk. "You can't afford to divorce."

The Knight of Cups scoots to the edge of his chair. "Don't worry about the finances. Just take care of the legalities."

He chuckles until his face flushes as red as his tie. "I don't know how you support a family a four on your salary."

"My husband works." I sit up straighter.

"His business has run a loss the past two years. That's not exactly adding to your income." He sits back and folds his hands over his stomach. "You do understand you'll have to pay spousal support for life. Not to mention child support until your daughter is eighteen. And until death for your son." He points to the Knight of Cups. "Your divorce was simple. You both made tons of money. This divorce can only take place with a miracle."

"How much money?" The Knight of Cups removes his checkbook.

Mr. Tyreck sits up and folds his hands on the desk. "My retaining fee is $5,000. My hourly is $350. I estimate the cost to dissolve this marriage is $15,000."

The Knight of Cups writes a check for the retaining fee and hands it to Mr. Tyreck.

I gape. Every muscle in my body tenses. Freedom from my marriage starts at five thousand dollars.

In the lobby, I tug on the Knight of Cups' shirt-sleeve. "I need to pay you back."

He shakes his head, wrapping an arm around my back. "You deserve to be rescued, my Cinderella."

Rescued? Outdated images of damsels in distress float through my mind. I twirl out of his embrace in the elevator and press my back against the wall. "Maybe I can work things out."

"I doubt that." He crosses his arms over his chest and nods to my feet. "When I filed for divorce from my wife, I waited until I was one hundred percent certain we couldn't work it out. Men aren't wishy-washy like women. Once a man makes up his mind, there is no turning back."

I hold out hope, coming home and making dinner and kissing you on the forehead. You flinch. "What was that for?"

"Just because." I smile.

"Did you have a fight with your boyfriend?"

I take a seat at the opposite end of the table. "Why don't we work things out?" I glance at our children flanking either side of us.

You narrow your gaze. "Why would I want to work things out with someone I no longer trust?"

"Because I'm the mother of your children." I broaden my smile and serve the rice. "I want to stay and work things out. We're a family."

Princess Pea stares at the mixed vegetables. "You used to steam fresh broccoli and cauliflower."

Forever Child knocks over his cup of juice and slams his fist against the table. He kicks his feet back and forth and bites his fingers.

I mop up the mess.

You glower. "You're a terrible wife and an awful mother."

"Dad's right." Princess Pea lifts her chin. "He's taking me to therapy to talk about you."

Even if I can't salvage my marriage, I can't let the Knight of Cups rescue me either. The next day, I head into the office of our onsite mortgage lender. I toss the same financial documents on her desk as I did the divorce attorney. "Can I qualify to buy my own place?"

"What are you looking for?"

I slump into the chair across from her desk. "Anything." My voice breaks. "I'm getting a divorce."

Later that afternoon, she calls me into her office.

She slides the envelope with my documents across the table. "I'm sorry, but even assuming you keep all of your income after the divorce, you only qualify for a purchase price of one hundred eighty thousand dollars."

That's a condo. As a real estate agent, I've been searching the listings for anything under two hundred thousand. I know I can't have a two story model, because Forever Child can't climb stairs. I also know I can't be located across from the pool or a busy street. Forever Child might disappear in the middle of the night and never be found alive again. That leaves only one condo available. By the time I submit an offer, the seller has accepted another one for twenty thousand dollars over the asking price.

Frustrated, I scan the online listings for rooms for rent. I need to stay in the same county during the divorce proceedings, so I can't take advantage of the offer of family in San Jose or San Francisco or Los Angeles.

On my lunch, I call three possibilities.

The first renter, a pleasant sounding woman, says she doesn't want to house anyone in transition.

"I'm not in transition. I'm stable. I've lived and worked here for over two decades. Why do you keep referring to me as being in transition?"

"You're divorcing. I don't want to deal with visiting children or new boyfriends or hostile family members."

Discouraged, I dial the other two numbers and leave messages.

By the end of the day, both renters have returned my calls. They also don't want to deal with a divorcing woman. They both would prefer to rent to college students or single professionals who have recently relocated to the area.

Near tears, I walk across the bank's parking lot. The sun blazes against my chest, and I blink my eyes.

The Knight of Cups hails me.

I wander over to the side of his truck.

"Let's get a drink," he says.

I glance at my watch. I've been coming home immediately after work as if the last six months have not happened. But pretending I didn't break what is clearly broken has not been working. "Just a few minutes. I have to go home and make dinner."

"No problem. We can meet at the burger joint."

I follow him out of the parking lot and drive the two miles away to park again. Inside, the air conditioning blasts against my face. I shiver. He orders two beers and some fries. We sit at the back of the restaurant on high stools at a tiny round table next to the floor-to-ceiling windows. He dips a fry into a bucket of ketchup and chews. "Any luck finding a place?"

Shaking my head, I take a sip of the sour beer. I push it aside. I can't risk smelling like alcohol as soon as I step inside. Rummaging in my purse, I pull out a package of gum and slide out a piece. Chomping on the minty strip, I inhale the intoxicating scent of peppermint and long for the days when I arrived home and relieved the sitter and fed the children and put them to bed and went to sleep alone before you unlocked the front door and slipped inside like a shadow. Closing my eyes briefly, I sigh. I don't care what I need to do. I just want to avoid one night of fighting.

He finishes his beer. "You know I have all that space." He shoves another fry in his mouth. "You could move in with me."

I widen my eyes and slide my beer toward him. "I—can't."

"Why not?" He sips from my mug and shrugs. "I'll charge you fifteen hundred dollars for renting one bedroom and one bathroom. Fair?"

I bow my head and twirl my fingers through the straps of my purse. Logically, this solution will end my worries about housing and money, at least temporarily. But emotionally, this offer feels too much like tightening the bonds between us too soon.

"I love you." He places his greasy, salty hand over mine.

I know the words falling from his mouth are sincere. But I've been in love countless times, and I know love is never enough.

"Please, move in with me." He curls his fingers over mine.

Should I?

I glance at my watch. Already fifteen minutes have passed. "I'll think about it." I stand, letting his hand fall to the side.

While I drive home, I turn the offer over in my mind like a worry stone.

Where else will I go?

I step inside the home, and Forever Child is tantruming for peanut butter and waffles. Princess Pea is hunched at the kitchen table trying to figure out how to write a geometry proof. The sitter is tugging at Forever Child's hand. You are bent over Princess Pea trying to explain each mathematical step.

No one notices me.

In the master bedroom, I slip out of my shoes and change into my home clothes—an old T-shirt and jeans. I tie back my long brown hair into a low pony tail and return to the kitchen. From the crisper drawer, I remove the fresh vegetables— kale, yellow onion, garlic, and mushrooms–and set the wooden cutting board on the counter. I dice the garlic and onion into one bowl. I slice the mushrooms and tear the kale from the stalks into quarter-sized pieces.

The sitter entices Forever Child out of the kitchen with music from a tablet.

Princess Pea nods with understanding and writes out the solution on college-ruled paper with her number two pencil.

You massage her shoulders. "I'm proud of you," you tell her.

She smiles up at you.

The two of you form a reflection.

I heat olive oil in a skillet on the gas stove. I never wanted this house. It was too old and boxy and hot with cinder block walls and a broken foundation. But the yard was over a quarter of an acre with room for a blow up pool and a swing set and a concrete patio large enough for a barbecue and picnic table and chairs. Inside, the bedrooms are tiny and the bathrooms even smaller. The rooms are heated with two wall heaters. We've swapped out the single paned windows for dual pane windows. We've remodeled the master bath and shower with custom tile we paid for with my real estate commissions. We've replaced the carpet with blond laminate flooring except the bedrooms. We've bought new furniture for the living room. We still have to buy a new garage door, remodel the children's bathroom, and the kitchen.

I never liked this house, but I will miss this home.

∾

THE NEXT CARD IN THE DINETTE READING REFERS TO how other people see me. Since I draw the Fool, a Major Arcana card, the opinions of others are beyond my control. The card depicts a housewife leaping over the rooftops with an open purse, the contents of which fly everywhere. Generally, the Fool refers to someone who has confidence and faith that things will work out. The person views the world with innocence and wonder and positivity. That person wants to live happily-ever-after. Since I am the Fool, drawing this card means others are seeing me clearly, as I am, maybe for the first time.

∼

YOU SUGGEST A MOVE OUT DATE OF SEPTEMBER 1, 2015. You want me to be around when the children start school in August.

In the middle of July, I attend an after work charity function with the Knight of Cups at Paradise Ridge Winery. We are representing the bank that has sponsored the event. The air is warm and the sunset is stunning with burgundy and burnt orange and streaks of neon pink. I am wearing a new sequined dress I purchased from JC Penney off the clearance rack for less than twenty dollars. My stacked heels and up do make me a half a foot taller so I reach his shoulders. A photographer from the *Press Democrat* snaps our picture.

You call me during the event, but I don't answer. You don't know I'm here with the Knight of Cups.

Or do you?

Our daughter's friend's mother is hosting the raffle. We used to go to their house and eat barbecue chicken and swim in the pool with our children. Now she waves me over, sizing up my date, and tells me she has filed for divorce from her husband of twenty years. "He wouldn't get a job while we were married, but two weeks after I filed, he's working full-time as the Vice President of Sales and Marketing for a big tech company." She shakes her head. "If he had just put in a little more effort, I wouldn't have asked him to move out. I wouldn't have filed."

"Is it too late?" I lean toward her.

A brass band is playing loud music outside. The notes float through the open doors and spiral around us.

She eyes my drink, then my man, before settling her gaze on me. "I wish I could, but he's already found a girlfriend—twenty years younger." She heaves a sigh and shakes her head. "Does your date have a brother?"

Without responding, I wander outside to the deck overlooking the steel "LOVE" sculpture in the vineyards that hundreds of couples have stood before to exchange their wedding vows. I find the woman's daughter—her eyes rimmed with charcoal eyeliner—standing by the band looking as lost as I feel. "I'm sorry about your parents' divorce."

She shrugs, turning a shoulder toward me, her gaze fixed on the sunset.

"You can talk to my daughter. Her father and I are also divorcing."

She shifts back toward me, an eyebrow arched. "Did her dad refuse to work too?"

I stiffen. You have always worked. After I got the job at the bank, I suggested you close your business and stay home with the children full-time, but you wanted to continue working. "No, he's always worked. We're divorcing because—"

"There you are." The Knight of Cups wraps an arm around my waist and draws me close. "I've been looking all over for you. That kind woman said you were out here talking to her daughter." He waves his drink toward the space in front of the band. "Do you want to dance?"

Without finishing my conversation, I join him on the dance floor.

We twirl around and laugh and smile—the picture perfect romantic couple.

The photographer from the *Press Democrat* snaps our photo again.

By the time I arrive home a little after 10 PM, you confront me at the front door. "Why didn't you answer?"

I shrug. "I couldn't hear my phone over all the noise."

"You could have called me on the drive home."

I narrow my gaze. You know I don't have a hands free device.

"Or sent a text message before you left." You sigh, run a hand through your thinning hair, and shake your head. "I was worried. You taught me how to worry. I don't want to worry about you anymore."

The next morning, you shake my shoulder and rustle the paper by my ear. "I thought you went alone to that work event." You stab a finger at the photograph of the Knight of Cups and me on the front page of the business section. "Do you know how humiliated I am?"

I cringe, burying my head under the pillow.

"I want you out by the end of the month."

The move out date is now August 1, 2015.

At work, someone has cut out the picture of me and the Knight of Cups and left it on my desk. No note. I scratch the back of my neck. At least we didn't kiss at the event. We didn't even hold hands. We only went dancing.

That afternoon, I receive a phone call from a woman I haven't seen in a couple of years. Our families met while shopping for shoes at Coddingtown Mall when our daughters were toddlers. She has a disabled daughter the same age as our disabled son. Over the years, we've exchanged advice and commiserated together and celebrated the tiny victories. One year, we even celebrated Thanksgiving together. She's seen my photo in the paper. She knows the man I am with is not my husband. "What's going on?" she asks.

I suggest we meet for lunch later in the week. "I'll explain everything," I say.

On the appointed day, we meet at a restaurant nearby. We sit outside beneath an umbrella for shade and order iced teas and salads.

"So, tell me what's going on?" She leans forward, batting her lashes.

I don't know if she's truly interested or just curious because she hasn't seen me in a while. I smooth the napkin on my lap and take a sip of the bitter iced tea before I launch into my story. I tell her everything from the tarot reader's prediction to the impending divorce and the upcoming move out date. As I talk, I watch her eyes widen, the corners of her mouth droop, the slope of her shoulders tighten. I am a morbid fascination, much like a car wreck on the side of the road, where people slow down to gawk, but not assist. I am an adulteress. My boyfriend is a home wrecker. Together we are every happy couple's worst nightmare.

Although she plies me for details—from how he kisses to where he lives—she never returns my calls again. She even blocks me on social media. When I ask you why she would take me out to lunch and then disappear, you reply, "She wanted to hear your cautionary tale. She has no interest in being friends with a traitor. Don't you know how contagious divorce is?"

I ask the Knight of Cups about his divorce experience.

"I didn't lose any friends. I gained all of my friends back," he says. "When I was married, my wife's friends became my friends. When we were raising children, our friends also had children. But during and after the divorce, I reconnected with the guys from high school and college who I hadn't spoken with for ten years. Divorce was a coming home for me."

But I don't see any "home" in any of this mess.

My friends and acquaintances all pull away from me.

I feel like a leper.

I feel so alone.

I feel like I no longer exist.

~

THE NEXT CARD IN THE DINETTE READING REFERS TO my past. Since I draw the Six of Swords, the past is struggling to reach an end, which means the past has lost its power to influence me. The card depicts a woman dressed in a coat, purse, and handheld luggage waving goodbye as she traipses across the handles of six knives. Three women's faces in silhouettes haunt the distance. I believe the three women represent the past, present, and future. Although the woman striding across the knives looks happy with a jaunt in her step, I feel less like a liberated woman and more like a satellite spinning out of orbit. The things I once held of value— you, our children, our marriage, our family—have fallen away. I am being forced to leave our home based on decisions I have made in the past. But I am not happy like the woman in the card. I am filled with regret. I am stark naked and vulnerable and scared, not stylish in a long cloak, white gloves, purse, and luggage waving goodbye with a Miss America smile, ready for whatever the future holds.

～

I HAVE NOT MOVED IN FIFTEEN YEARS. I AM surprised by how much I have accumulated. More than just the average person of new clothes, shoes, and books, I also house a lifetime of memories in baby photographs, report cards, award ribbons, and pen pal letters yellowed with age. I wade through my entire life, determining what I will take with me to the Knight of Cups' house and what I will dispose of in the recycling or trash.

Sometimes Princess Pea joins me. She sits cross-legged on the carpet, fingering the items in the discard pile—mostly love letters from you over the years. She reads them with the same interest she reads her English assignments for school, pausing to look up words she doesn't know and writing down thoughts that occur to her for a later discussion. By the time I gather up the letters to haul them to the blue recycling can outside, she places her cool fingers against my arm. "Why are you getting rid of the evidence that Daddy loves you?"

She is a budding forensic scientist. She attended a summer training program at the local university on a scholarship and watches the First 48, a behind-the-scenes investigation of real life homicides, religiously. What I see as starting over, she sees as destroying evidence for an event that happened, an event with lasting consequences that extend beyond this present moment, perhaps as far as all time.

Even your sister sees value in everything I am eager to discard. "Your divorce isn't final. You might need something to present to the court," she says, from the practical side. "You're a writer. You might need to reference these letters if you decide to write about the divorce someday."

I have no intention of writing about the divorce. My only intention is making a clean break, of dissolving the past twenty-five years of my life. I have no use for any of the two recycling cans full of evidence. I am looking forward to starting a new life—not a new chapter but a whole new book—with the Knight of Cups. I am eager to move into the four bedroom house he shares with his rescue dog and his three teenage children who occasionally stay over.

Every day after work and every weekend, I

struggle to consolidate all of my belongings into three plastic tubs—mostly collectibles, awards, and a few essential papers, such as tax returns and publishing contracts. Additionally, I will be taking my books, art supplies, paintings, and the laptop your mother bought me for Christmas. I decide to keep one memento from the years we've been together—the first greeting card you bought me. On the outside, a tiny red heart smiles. Inside, the message reads, "That's all I had to say." At your request, I have not taken any photographs, not even my favorite picture of Princess Pea and me at preschool which hangs from a magnet on the refrigerator door. I am leaving all the furniture too, except the bookcase you built for me and the dresser I have had since I was six years old. Everything else—the kitchen appliances, our marital bed, the household furniture, the children—are yours.

A week before our twenty-third wedding anniversary and two weeks before my forty-fourth birthday, I receive a call from the movers. "We're still at a house in Marin," the guy says. "We'll call you when we get ready to leave here, okay?"

A jolt of panic spikes my blood. What option do I have? I don't want the Knight of Cups transporting my belongings. I am afraid of a confrontation between you and him.

An hour later, the moving company calls again. "We're stopping in Tiburon to move a family to Novato since it's on the way back. We promise you're next."

Already the sun is blazing in the midday sky. I

don't want to wait all day. I grab my clothes and shove them into the backseat of my car and stow my art supplies in the trunk and drive over to the Knight of Cups' house.

Inside, he guides me into the office and points to the tiny closet against the wall. "You can put your stuff here. My closet is too small." I place my laptop on the desk by the window and hang the dresses and slacks in the mirrored closet and stack the art supplies in a corner. I sigh with frustration. His house is more than twice the size of the one I am leaving, and yet I will have to trek several feet from the master bedroom to the office every day to get dressed for work.

For the first time since I began packing, a trickle of doubt runs along my spine. I drive back to the marital home and wonder if I am making a mistake. Should I stay and try once again to work things out with you?

In the time I have been gone, you have moved all of the boxes of books, the three plastic tubs, my bookcase, and my dresser onto the front lawn. The neighbors have come by to ask what is going on and you have told them the truth—I am abandoning the family to start a new life with another man.

I park along the curb and gape at the public display. Shame douses the anger rising from my skin. I duck inside the house and wait.

As the hours tick by, I wonder if I will have to ask you to move all the boxes back into the house and reschedule the move for the following weekend.

By the time the sun crests behind the house

and my stomach growls, hungry for dinner, I finally receive a call. "Do you still need us?" the guy asks.

"Yes, of course, I do. Why wouldn't I?"

"I just thought you might have gotten tired of waiting."

I have, but I don't tell him that.

"We're on our way."

You follow me outside and stand beside me with your hands on your hips and a smug smile on your face. "Once you leave, you can never come back."

The finality of those words hits my gut. *Never come back*. I swallow, pivot away. I don't want you to see the tears in my eyes.

Twenty-five years ago I left my parents' house in San Jose and moved to Santa Rosa to be with you. I never returned to my parents' house except to visit.

Today, I leave our house of fifteen years to live with a man I have been dating for only four months although I have worked with him for four years. I will return every other weekend to care for our children. But once I leave I am no longer your responsibility. I will belong to someone else.

You take a step closer. "You can stay." Your voice taps my back. "You can break up with your boyfriend and return to the family." Your voice touches my shoulder, a caress. "You can quit your job. You never have to see him again." The words trickle down my spine. "I'll find work so you can write and be with the kids. I'll even take care of them so you can go on that nationwide book tour in October." The words pool at the base of my spine, strong and warm. "We can rebuild our lives and be a family again."

A truck honks.

I glance up, startled.

The moving truck lumbers into the driveway.

I step aside, the words falling away, the heat of your promises gone.

Two guys jump out of the cab and roll up the back of the truck. They survey the items on the lawn.

The taller, leaner guy waves an arm across the piles. "Is this it?"

I nod.

"We should have come here first."

Anger and frustration bristle across my shoulders. Yes, of course, they should have. But they didn't. And I spent all day wavering back and forth, a teeter totter of hope and doubt, swaying like a branch in the wind, wondering if I should stay or go.

You reach out one last time. "You don't have to leave."

But I do. I've come too far.

Without a kiss or a hug goodbye, I withdraw my keys and slip into the hot front seat of my car. After starting the engine, I lead the moving truck across town to my new residence.

Within ten minutes, the two guys have unloaded all of my belongings and set them on the floor of the family room. There is so much space surrounding me that I feel my life has shrunk to the small mountain before me. I've left so much behind.

The Knight of Cups surveys the stack of books,

the dresser, the bookcase, and the plastic tubs. He waves to one wall. "Your bookcase can go here." He points to the plastic tubs and nods to the office. "You can stack those in the closet beneath your clothes." He opens one of the six boxes of books and gasps. "You didn't tell me you're a hoarder."

A hoarder? I throw my arms out wide. "I am not a hoarder. I am a writer. Books are my tools."

He tears open all six boxes of books and scoffs. "You're a hoarder. Why don't you just rent books from the library like everyone else?" He points to three slim volumes on one of the built in bookcases flanking the brick fireplace against the back wall. "Those books were gifts. I read them once. I'll never read them again."

A cold sensation plunges through me. This man does not know me. How can I share my life with him? The realization prickles across my scalp, and I shudder. I have made a mistake. Picking up a book, I flip through the pages. "I read this book once a year. It makes me laugh. Why go to the library every year for a book that might be checked out by someone else when I can just pull it off my bookshelf and read it right now?" I stride over to another box and remove another book. "This book I use in my memoir writing class. I've highlighted passages and written notes in the margins. I can't do that with a library book." Finally, I stoop to pick up an old leather-bound book with thin yellow pages that smell of must and wisdom. I turn to the opening pages and point to the scrawled words inside. "This book has been signed by the author. It's a first edition. Very valuable. Worth more than all the jewelry I own. There's special rider on my insurance policy that covers the financial loss in the event the book is stolen or destroyed in a fire." I hug the book to my chest like a dear friend. "I'm *not* a hoarder. These books are my life. I will not part with them."

The muscles around his mouth twitch. He jabs a finger at the bookcase you built for me. "All those books won't fit."

"I know." Back in the marital home, I double or triple stacked volumes like nested Russian dolls. Now I point to the gleaming white built in bookcases behind me. "I thought I could display the rest of my books there."

He sweeps his gaze across the framed photographs of his three children in different ages and his framed prints of Van Gogh and three lone volumes on the otherwise empty shelves. "We'll talk about that later. I'm hungry. Let's go out to eat."

I don't remember where we went or what we ate, but I do remember coming home and turning on my laptop and asking for the password to the router. I remember logging into my social media account to change the status of my relationship from "married" to "separated." Scrolling through the posts, I notice the message on your page:

And then there were three.

A picture of you, Forever Child, and Princess Pea sitting around the dining room table graces the caption. A sharp pain stabs my chest, and I log off before I can type a nasty reply.

But inside all the edges are poking into tender flesh.

After a long moment, I decide to call my mother and tell her the news.

"What have you done?" she yells down the line. "Go home and be a good wife and mother. Tell that other man you never want to see him again." She heaves a sigh and lowers her voice. "Did I ever tell you about the customer at the bank who brought me flowers every week? He asked me to leave your father and move to Los Angeles with him. But he didn't want me to take my children with me. You were ten, and your sisters were seven and almost six. No matter how much I fought with your father or how much I loved the other man, I could not abandon you and your sisters. So I stayed and learned to fall in love with your father again."

I break down in tears. "My boyfriend wouldn't let me bring my children. I have to go back to the old house to take care of them every other weekend."

"Of course you do," she says, her voice rising once again. "No man wants to raise another man's children."

I don't know why I never spoke with my mother before about my relationship with the Knight of Cups. If I had, do you think her wisdom would have saved us?

"Go home," my mother says once again. "Make things right with your husband."

But I can't.

You made that clear before I jangled my keys and started the engine of my car.

Once I leave, I can never come back.

I end the call. Disappointment hangs like a

mantle against my shoulders. I pad across the house, dragging my feet. All throughout my childhood my mother screamed and yelled and complained, hiding her love affair beneath a hostile exterior, shielding my sisters and me from the brutalities of romantic love and the harsh realities of raising a family. Why didn't she share her experiences with me before I married? What use was her confession after I had already inflicted damage on my family?

In the kitchen, the Knight of Cups is drinking vodka and diet soda and watching the news. I sidle up beside him, and he wraps his arm around me absently, his gaze still transfixed by the TV screen. The dog lopes up behind me, burying her nose against my legs, looking for affection. I am allergic to dogs. I couldn't have one as a child for long because I always ended up with perpetual cold-like symptoms—runny nose and teary eyes. I've planned ahead, doubling up on my prescription medication. But I don't know if those precautions will be enough.

"Do you like your new home?" the Knight of Cups asks.

I glance around the kitchen. The layout is functional with a stovetop island and plenty of counter space. The room flows into the dining and living rooms in an open floor plan. But I didn't spend ten years saving for the down payment. I don't own anything, from the dishes in the cabinets to the area rugs on the hardwood floors.

I am a tenant. Not a homeowner.

I am a girlfriend. Not a wife.

I am a mother who has abandoned her children.

How will I fit into this new life?

~

THE NEXT CARD IN THE DINETTE READING REFERS TO my hopes and fears. I draw the Eight of Cups. On the card, a woman with a hand across her forehead frowns at two stacks of eight tea cups. She looks emotionally exhausted. No wonder—the Suit of Cups refers to emotions.

In a love reading, the Eight of Cups refers to soul-searching. What brings one joy, contentment, and fulfillment? A few tarot readers interpret the Eight of Cups as the card of disillusionment. The reality of the situation is not as good as one believed it would be. Other tarot readers suggest this card indicates walking away from a situation regardless of whether or not one ends up with regrets.

I have already walked away from my marriage. I have faced the disillusionment of my living situation with the Knight of Cups. How much more soul-searching must I do before I discover joy, contentment, and fulfillment?

~

EVERY OTHER WEEKEND, I RETURN TO THE HOME I once shared with you to take care of our children. You stay somewhere else. I don't ask where you go or who you spend your time with. Your life is your own now.

In the house we once shared, the photographs

have been stripped from the walls. The only thing remaining is the black and white dragon you sketched with a number two pencil and framed above the TV cabinet in the living room. I don't know where our wedding photograph went. I don't know where the photograph of Princess Pea and me resides. For all I know, you could have torn them both to pieces or thrown them in the trash.

The door to the master bedroom is now locked with a key.

You have unplugged the cord to the TV so I can't binge watch romantic comedies while folding a week's worth of laundry on the black sofa.

Painful reminders of the life I have left behind gape from every room, from the stove where you and your best friend fried tilapia for Mother's Day to the honey-do-list on the refrigerator where I've listed every home repair that needs to be made to the laminate flooring you installed to the big back-yard with the endless yard you would spend each weekend mowing to the black sofa where we sat as a family playing Rock Band with you on the guitar, Princess Pea on vocals, and Forever Child and I banging on the drums. Ghosts rise up from behind your black chair where you sat every night on your laptop and the ottoman where I perched beside your feet talking about the events of the day or the burdens in my heart. The empty walls scream of my absence where once I would rotate the paintings to match the seasons. Every creak in the laminate flooring triggers memories of walking up and down the hallway to chase our son in the middle of the night. Our children's rooms remain unchanged except for a futon against one wall in our daughter's room where I sleep, tossing and turning on the lumpy mattress, wondering how I will get some rest in a house haunted with memories.

When I ask the Knight of Cups if I can have my children visit on the weekends, he says he only wants me—no one else. I remind him he also has children. He reminds me they live at their mother's house.

At the marital home, I sit at the kitchen table, the first real piece of furniture I purchased for three thousand dollars, and mourn the loss of the sleek blond wood I would polish once a week. My fingers trace a few scratches and pen marks that were never there when I was here. Tears spark at the backs of my eyes.

Without anything to distract from a house full of memories, I drink whatever cheap, high-alcohol booze I can buy from the corner liquor store. I hide the bottles in my overnight bag and take regular sips throughout the day, hoping to blur the edges of my unhappiness so the pain becomes only background noise.

But Princess Pea smells my sour breath. She tells you I am drinking.

"If you keep that up, you'll lose your visits," you threaten.

I pour out the booze, crush the cans, and pretend to comply.

But as soon as the vigilance softens, I start up again.

On the weekends I do not have our children I

wake before the first streak of dawn, slather sunscreen over my body, and dress in the uniform my boyfriend bought me to match his orange and black softball jersey. I order a customized baseball cap with "Crush Girl" embroidered in loopy script and tug my pony tail out of the hole in the back. Sitting shotgun, I ride to whatever out-of-town location the current tournament is located— Pleasanton, Redwood City, Sacramento, or Reno. As the sun sneaks past the horizon, I zip up a sweatshirt against the crisp chill and watch his teammates and him practice batting and catching on a neighboring soccer field before the game starts.

In the bleachers, I sit next to the teammates' wives who have been attending these softball tournaments for up to thirty years. They gaze at me with kind suspicion. I don't ask how many other women have come to these events as a guest. I smile and listen to their questions and ask about the rules of the game.

When a fly ball or home run barrels over the chain link fence, I bolt up and run after the ball. The umpire flashes a smile, accepting my toss, and winks. "That's our Crush Girl," he says.

After the games, the team gathers in the parking lot for beer and refreshments.

I mill around, sipping on sour beer and nibbling on chips. The guys slap each other's shoulders or jab each other's ribs and complain of aches and pains along their backs and down their legs. The wives smile and look like pretty flowers wilting in the heat of the late afternoon sunshine. I never was part of the popular crowd in high school, but I imagine these informal gatherings mirror the same camaraderie of those sporting events minus the illicit alcohol and smoking, which are permitted at this late age.

During the week, I attend more softball games on Mondays and Wednesdays.

On Tuesdays and Fridays, the Knight of Cups suggests joining a bowling league.

I have not bowled in years.

He buys me shoes, and I try out the size and heft of the balls stacked along the wall.

The bowling alley is brightly lit and full of older couples and singles who have bowled together for years. The musty recycled air stinks like the inside of a sweaty locker room mingled with the greasy scent of pizza and sour booze from the snack bar and lounge. A karaoke contest is underway in the bar, and the jagged refrains of out of tune singers grate against the piped in music in the bowling alley.

My parents bowled in a league during the early years of their marriage. When my mother returned to work after my sisters and I started elementary school, she joined her company's Wednesday night bowling league. Both of my parents were great bowlers. Bronze statues lined the fireplace mantle.

I am not.

When the Knight of Cups introduces me to the two players on our team, he places his hand on my lower back.

"My, you're pretty," his best friend and team captain says. "The Knight of Cups deserves a pretty girlfriend."

Something about the man reminds me of you. Maybe it is his sense of humor. Maybe it is his blue eyes.

The teams are pitted against each other, playing three games a night. Whichever team scores the highest number of overall points wins.

I stand before the lane and aim the ball, take three steps, swing my arm back, and release the ball against the gleaming wood. The ball barrels down the lane and veers into the gutter. On my second try, I pick off one pin.

By the end of the first game, I've only scored 79 points.

Everyone else on our team has bowled at least double.

The highest bowler has scored 190 points.

When someone bowls over 200, the lights flash overhead and an announcer behind the counter says, "On lane number eight, Tina Marie has bowled 201 points. Give it up for Tina Marie!"

The room erupts in cheers.

Rounds of beers are bought and drank.

By the end of the evening, with my joints lubricated from one too many beers, I bowl a game of just over 100.

The Knight of Cups wraps his arm around my shoulder. "Don't worry about how you play," he says. "You give our team a big handicap, which will help in the playoffs."

But as I walk out of the stuffy bowling alley and into the dark, cooling night, I can't help but wonder about the life I left behind.

Even though you never played in any tournament sports or bowled with me, you taught me how to run and lift weights, building up my body instead of tearing it down with fast food and alcohol. When the children were younger, we would go to the high school track on early mornings and take turns running laps. Sometimes Princess Pea would join us. Forever Child always sank to his knees and yanked fistfuls of grass. Afterward, we came home and cooked eggs and squeezed fresh juice from the bag of oranges picked off my parents' tree which they left for us after a weekend visit. We never ate greasy, salty breakfast sandwiches from the drive- through or drank mimosas or Bloody Mary's.

After I wake up with a pounding headache and heavy limbs and a blank slate that slowly brightens with images from last night, I pad into the kitchen and brew coffee from the coffee maker I bought after moving here and sip the hot liquid sludge, wishing for those mornings with you and our family.

To make matters worse, the constant binge drinking and fast food eating pack twenty pounds onto my short frame. Staring at my reflection, I don't recognize myself. I weigh exactly what I did when I was nine months pregnant. My lumpy body is hard on my joints when I run, and none of my clothes fit. When I call Scott, hoping he will go shopping with me, his cell phone has been disconnected. I send an email and receive a brief reply.

—I let the cell phone go. I'm busy remodeling my house. Maybe we can have lunch or talk next week.—

But next week comes and goes without lunch or talking.

The only person maintaining regular contact

with me is a guy I met at the gym, a person who I thought would only ever be an acquaintance I would chat with during my thirty minutes on the elliptical machine.

But this overweight, middle-aged man has been divorced and has recovered from alcohol abuse. He warns me of the dangers I am entering. "I lost everything. You have to do your best to get sober. You have to be fully prepared to fight. You can't be drunk and negotiate. I don't want you to end up like me—broke and unhappy and alone."

I promise him I won't. But I can't keep that promise.

Once, long ago, I drank daily for nine months after breaking up with an on-again, off-again lover. The grief I felt over choosing you over him left me with a gaping hole. I mourned the loss of who I was with him—a single, successful writer—instead of embracing who I was with you—a loving wife and mother. Only once I became pregnant with Princess Pea did I decide to get sober.

I was sober for fifteen years.

Now drinking has become a way of life. I can't imagine a day without it.

One weekend when I am with the children I drink too much. Princess Pea finds me passed out on the futon in the middle of the day. She brings me water and helps me sit up to drink. "You need to get better, Mommy. We need you."

My head aches, and my body shudders. I wrap the thin blanket around my shoulders and squint in the too bright afternoon light. "What time is it?"

"Time for you to make dinner."

I am too drunk to drive, and I have not

brought any food to cook this time. The refrigerator is always bare when I arrive.

Finding my phone in the covers, I dial the Knight of Cups. "I need help. I'm drunk. I don't have any food for the kids. Can you help?"

Within an hour, the Knight of Cups delivers a full dinner for us. He has barbecued chicken and steamed mixed vegetables and made prepackaged rice.

He glances around the space, at the laundry piled on the black sofa, at the dishes in the kitchen sink, at the sadness tugging at the corners of my mouth, at the hungry stares of my children. He turns and leaves.

I've never felt so alone in my life.

But I am grateful for the sustenance.

When I return to his home on Sunday night, he greets me in the kitchen. "We have to talk about your drinking." He sips from a tall glass of vodka and diet soda. "You can't drink when you take care of your kids. I might have a softball game and not be here to respond to your call. You need to step up to the plate and be a mom."

"*Now* you want me to be a mother?" I throw my arms wide open. "All this time you've said you don't want anything to do with my children."

"I don't." He hardens his mouth into a thin line. "But that doesn't mean you get to abandon your responsibilities because you're with me. That's not very attractive, you know?"

I heave a sigh. I don't know who I am anymore or who I need to be or who I want to become. I only know I am not sufficient as is. I am a bad mother. I am an irresponsible drunk. I am woman who abandoned her family to go live with someone else to begin a shiny, new life.

But this life isn't shiny or new anymore.

Finally, that guilt and remorse I should have felt after betraying you three times surface.

I want to ask your forgiveness.

I miss our old, simple life.

I want to leave this overgrown frat boy with a fat wallet.

I want to come home.

The counselor I've returned to seeing, the one I saw when I was struggling in my marriage to you all those years ago, says I should stay where I am with the Knight of Cups. "You can't afford to return to a narcissist."

"But he's not a narcissist." I am sitting across from her on the pale sofa that blends into the walls. "He's lost tons of weight because he can't keep food down. He's miserable without me. He cries every day." I ball up my hands and inhale deeply the incense-infused air. "I feel bad for leaving him and our children. I want to go home."

She leans forward, her trick leg trembling against the staff she uses for walking, and clasps her hands between her knees. "I think the man you're with is kindhearted."

"Why?" I grab a tissue and blot the corners of my eyes.

"He ran into the kitchen to tell you a blue jay had taken the doves' eggs from the nest beneath the window. He was shaken with shock and grief. How can you leave a man like that?"

I shake my head, recalling that story I told her. I was standing in the kitchen blending my protein shake in a crappy, ten dollar blender I bought at a discount store when he grabbed my shoulders and pointed to the window overlooking the backyard. Moisture gleamed in his blue eyes. He rattled on and on about how he couldn't rescue the doves' eggs when the blue jay snatched them from the nest. He was disappointed in his inability to prevent the sudden loss.

She clasps her hands to her chest and sighs. "A man who cares for doves' eggs will care for you."

Frowning, I lean back against the squishy cushions. Just because he admires the doves who mate for life does not mean he will want to mate with me for life. After all, he has already divorced the mother of his three children. Regardless of the reason, the fact remains—he is not one of the ten percent of mammals who are faithfully monogamous. He may be a serial monogamist, preferring one female at a time, but he is not a dove. He will not come back to the same nest every year to make a new family with the same woman. And, frankly, I don't know if I am that type of person either. After all, if I was, I wouldn't be here, sitting in my therapist's office, discussing an illicit love affair that has led to an impending divorce.

The therapist checks the time. "We're almost at the end of our session. I want you to be strong. I understand you can be sympathetic to your husband's emotions, but I don't want you to fall under his spell and be manipulated again." She shakes her head and thins her lips. "I've witnessed you experience too much heartbreak. Now you have an opportunity to start over with another man." She leans forward and holds my gaze. "I want you to seriously consider this option. Understand?"

I nod, thinking of all the other things she is not saying, even if she may be thinking them. That this other man does not welcome my two children into his heart or his home. That this other man does not believe in a god, especially not the God who has sent me to him. That this other man's idea of health and fitness is playing in senior softball tournaments every other weekend and drinking beer and eating pizza. That this other man does not read and considers me a hoarder since I own more books than I do shoes or clothes. That this other man does not really know me.

How can I give up what I have with my husband who has grown up with me and sacrificed his whole life to raising our children, loving them so much, especially our son, who is so fragile and disabled, no matter how damaged, broken, or worn-out our marriage might be? Can't the therapist see my boyfriend is no better than the blue jay, stealing something that is not rightfully his? Or is my therapist a naturalist, taking into consideration only the cycle of life and the hierarchy of the food chain? Whoever is the strongest, biggest, fastest, or richest must triumph in the end, no morality involved? And since my boyfriend is richer and stronger than my husband, the boyfriend will naturally win.

Leaving with more questions than answers, I step into the heat of late September, breathe in deeply, and glance at the sky. Is there any rational explanation for a man who can cry over the loss of a doves' family, yet insists on breaking up a human family?

A few days later, my boyfriend's youngest daughter has a high school dance recital. I am invited to attend. While waiting for the lights to dim and the curtain to rise, I meet the ex-wife, a petite brunette with kind brown eyes and a wide smile.

As soon as my boyfriend leaves to use the restroom, she tells me a story I have heard before about the birth of my boyfriend's first son. But her version is slightly different, colored by the perspective of time and womanhood. "He was on the softball field playing when I was admitted to the hospital. I paged him. He slid into the delivery room and donned a hospital gown and gloves just moments before an emergency C-section. He held up our son like he was the hero of the day." She tightens her smile when my boyfriend returns. "I was just telling your girlfriend about the day Stanley was born."

He smiles. "Ah, yes, it was the bottom of the ninth and I was up to bat. I hit a homerun, winning the game for the team. We were on our way to the pizza joint when I got the 911 page." He puffs out his chest and smiles. "I made it in time for the birth."

That night, I can't sleep. I keep thinking about the birth of our son. How I was sent home after the first signs of labor and told to walk a few miles until the contractions made it impossible to walk anymore. You were with me the entire time, circling the block over and over. When we returned to the hospital, I was dilated five centimeters. Within a couple of hours, I was dilated three more. By the time the pain peaked, I screamed for some relief, and a nurse injected something into my blood stream. I calmed down so much I fell asleep. I had to be woken an hour later to push.

When our son arrived, you held his capped and swaddled body and offered him to me.

I shook my head, too tired and worn out.

But you insisted, opening my arms gently, and settling the baby between them.

Our son glowered at me with a furrowed brow and dark eyes. He was round and heavy like a bowling ball. He cried when the blonde nurse left the room.

"Take him back." I lifted him in my arms.

You whisked him up and nestled him close to your neck, the length of his body firm against your chest.

The cries snuffled into the soft breaths of sleep.

Even after our son was diagnosed with all of his disabilities, you still held him close, you still calmed him to sleep.

In the morning, before leaving for work, I swipe the screen on my phone and call you.

The mail box is full and cannot receive any messages.

I send a text.

—*I miss you. Let's call off the divorce.*—

After I drive to the bank and park, I check my phone.

No messages.

You live only five minutes away. I consider the time—ten minutes till I need to clock into work. I could pay you a visit, knock on the door, let myself in with the key I still have.

But then I remember you're not home. You're in your car driving Princess Pea to school.

The nagging feeling to return to you continues to burn like a smoldering flame. I drive home from church on Sunday with the window rolled down. The wind whips my hair around my face, fanning the flames of longing. At a traffic light, I roll up the window and the rush of air stills into silence. I press the number for our home phone and listen to the steady ringing until someone picks up.

After your greeting, I say, "I've missed you."

"I've been sick with a cold."

You don't sound sick. But I pull into the parking lot of the nearest grocery store and purchase a pint of hot chicken noodle soup from the deli. The container warms my hands, and I buoy with hope.

A few minutes later, I pull into the driveway and park beside your car like I have always done. I carry the hot container of chicken noodle soup in my hands and ring the doorbell.

When you answer, you let me inside.

You are wearing a T-shirt and sweat pants. Your hair is messy. Crusts of sleep crease the corners of your blue eyes.

"I brought you soup. Do you need me to take care of the children so you can sleep?"

You stare at my peace offering. "Thanks, but I'm feeling better." You nod to the front door. "You should go. Your boyfriend is probably waiting for you."

I recoil. That man I live with may have become my boyfriend but I do not want to be with him anymore.

You hold open the front door.

Even from this distance, I can smell the faint whiff of your woodsy cologne. The strands of nostalgia and longing braid up the backs of my legs and tighten the muscles. I don't want to go. "May I see the children?" I place the container of soup on the kitchen table.

"Princess Pea is working on homework and Forever Child is in his room. I prefer you leave and not upset them. They'll see you next weekend."

Your gaze is firm.

"Didn't you get my message?" I point to your cell phone on the coffee table. "I want to work things out."

"You should have thought about that before you moved out." You grab your phone. "Do I need to call the police and get a restraining order?"

Anger pulverizes through me. I stomp out of the house.

You slam the door.

My body convulses with tears.

Alone, in my car, I turn the key and start the engine. I remember telling you, months ago, about a woman at work whose husband of thirty years brought her fresh coffee whenever he drove by the bank. He worked as a shuttle driver for a dealership, taking people to various destinations throughout the day while their vehicles were being serviced.

After I started dating the Knight of Cups, you

stopped by the bank, dressed in your three-piece suit to deliver a store-bought mocha. I remember the receptionist calling me to the front desk. Co-workers' curious stares followed me as I walked down the hallway. When I returned to my desk with the mocha, but not you, the co-workers' disappointment was reflected in their gazes.

What did they know about you then that I know about you now?

The store-bought mocha was a grand romantic gesture to win back my love and affection.

But I accepted the gesture and rejected you.

On the drive back to my boyfriend's house, I turn up the radio and listen to Taylor Swift sing, "Shake It Off." I no longer tap my fingers against the steering wheel or sing along with the lyrics. I snap off the radio and stew in silence.

Is this how you felt that morning, arriving generous and hopeful in your three-piece suit and store-bought mocha? Is this how you felt on the drive home, humiliated and bitter and alone?

Minutes later, I park along the street beside my boyfriend's house, his truck hogging both spaces in the driveway. I am certain I have made a mistake. I have left the wrong person. I have let the blue jay steal my eggs and rob me of my family and my home.

～

THE NEXT CARD IN THE DINETTE READING REFERS TO how I see myself. I draw the reversed Queen of Cups. In tarot, cards drawn with the image upside down are called reversals. Reversals contain the same energy present in the upright card although that energy may be blocked or stifled. Reversals can also signify the exact opposite meaning of the card in the upright position. Using both of these interpretations, the Queen of Cups reversed can either portray a woman who lacks love and caring or whose love and caring are blocked either by self-imposed or external obstacles. Since the Queen of Cups in an upright position symbolizes love, caring, and emotional security, I believe drawing this reversal illuminates the exact opposite characteristics. After all, I'm the mother who abandoned her children, the wife who left for another man, and the woman who broke free from the emotional security of home. But if I can right the wrongs in my life, maybe I can overturn this reversal and once again become the caring mother, the adoring wife, and the faithful woman who offers the loving stability of home.

~

DAYS LATER, MY BOYFRIEND WAKES EARLY, HOOKS me in his arms, and asks, "May I come along on your book tour?"

The length of my body chills and stiffens against his naked warmth. The trip, which I coordinated with a handful of fans and a publicist, was scheduled six months ago. At the time, I planned on traveling across country alone.

He must interpret the expression on my face as one of resistance, because he tightens his grip against me and adds, "I'll pay my own way...and carry your bags."

Oh, how tempting. I wriggle against his embrace. I still suffer from that back injury from the warehouse accident, and I can't lift or carry anything heavier than ten pounds. Having him with me will allow me to pack more and bring back more.

"We can sight see between book signings. It can be our first trip together." He buries his nose against the nape of my neck. "I want to spend the rest of my life making memories with you."

I don't know what to say, so I don't say anything at all.

When I confide my concerns with the receptionist at work, she says, "Traveling together will bring you closer or tear you both apart. It's a great litmus test for a relationship."

I march into his office and place the dates on his desk. "If you want to go, you'll need to request time off for the last week of October. I'll see if I can book your seats next to me on the same flight, or if I'll have to cancel and rebook the itinerary. I only have one layover day in Washington, D.C. If you want to site see, we can visit the capital. Otherwise, it's flight, bookstore, reading or presentation, and flight for seven days."

He glances at the piece of paper on his desk. A slow smile spreads across his face.

Sighing, I hope the receptionist is right, and I'll return from the trip with a clear resolution to this untenable situation—can I make this relationship work with the Knight of Cups or will I have to find a way to strike out on my own?

A week before the trip, I pack my outfits—the red and gold cheongsam with the embroidered dragon snaking from my shoulder to my thighs, a new, fluffy, white cardigan, gray slacks and several blouses, black boots, sneakers, and various undergarments. In my computer bag, I stuff a marked up copy of my book with the passages I will read and notes for my school presentations.

I send a text to you.

—*Leaving next week for the book tour. I'll post every day on my blog.*—

You send back a response.

—*Okay. Please also let me know when you arrive safely at each destination.*—

I agree, but I neglect to inform you I am traveling with the Knight of Cups.

On the morning of the first flight from San Francisco to Virginia, the Knight of Cups and I arrive at the airport at a quarter to five in the morning. The sky is dark. The air is crisp and cool. I am dressed in the outfit I will wear that night at the reading. My black overcoat is draped across my shoulders even though no snow is expected during our stay in Virginia. We won't be renting a car until we reach the Midwest, so we will be relying on public transportation to get us from the airport to the hotel to One Page Books where I'm scheduled to read at seven.

Having only flown three times in my life, I don't budget any extra lead time for delays or mechanical failures or any other possibility. I anticipate each flight to go as scheduled.

But everything that could go wrong does.

Our first flight from San Francisco is delayed. We leave one hour later than scheduled.

Arriving in Chicago, we experience a layover that lasts forty-five minutes longer than it should because of the plane's engine troubles.

By the time we arrive in Dulles International

Airport, we have forty-five minutes to travel from the airport to the bookstore.

The taxi driver says he'll do his best to get us there on time, but he can't promise anything in this bumper-to-bumper traffic.

The maze of cars snakes through arteries of highway, reminiscent of the days when you commuted from San Jose to Mountain View before we moved to Santa Rosa in 1990. I glance at my watch and feel a spike of panic. Fumbling with my cell phone, I call One More Page Books and speak with the event manager.

"You should be fine," she says. "Without traffic, the drive is only twenty minutes. If you're late, I'll stall the audience with a trivia game and a drawing."

Thankful, I end the call and remember to breathe.

Because I don't want to fuel my anxiety, I don't gaze out the window. I focus on calming the racing thoughts in my mind, the ones that breed disaster. When that strategy does not work, I send you a text.

—*Arrived over two hours late. Might not make it to the bookstore in time.*—

Within moments, my phone pings.

—*Don't worry. God will make sure you get there on time.*—

"Who are you texting?" The Knight of Cups looks over my shoulder.

Without responding, I tuck the phone into my purse.

Instead of pressing for details, he grabs my hand and squeezes it until the blood returns and my fingers warm. "You'll do fine. We'll get dinner afterward to celebrate."

But I don't feel fine. I am frayed with nerves. I had planned on arriving early enough to check into the hotel and eat before driving to the venue. Now I will be lucky if I arrive before the audience gets bored of waiting and leaves.

Then, without explanation, the sky darkens.

Big, fat, gray raindrops splatter against the windows. The taxi driver turns on the wipers, and they fan across the glass, back and forth, like hands waving across the room to someone important who has just stepped inside but who can't see through the crowd. The knot in my stomach tightens, and the nervous energy buzzing in my body finds release in the tapping of my fingers against my gray, wool slacks. I'm wearing the black and white striped clown sweater since the Knight of Cups said it would be good luck. I'm hoping he's right. I need all the luck I can get right now.

With five minutes to spare, the taxi driver pulls up to the front of the tiny bookstore on an otherwise dark street. The Knight of Cups grabs our suitcases and pays the driver while I thread my arms through the backpack and dart to the door. The whoosh of cold rain sprinkles against my cheeks followed by the dry warmth of the store with its welcoming lights and new paper smells.

The event manager asks, "Are you the author speaking tonight?"

"Yes, I am."

She whisks me away, into a room in the back, where I can use the restroom and have a glass of water before she introduces me.

In the tiny alcove, I stand between boxes of books and a desk with a computer near the doorway and listen to her speak. When I hear my name, I grasp my book and stride into the store.

Three rows of chairs face a small desk and a microphone.

I take a seat and open my book.

The Knight of Cups stands by the cash register with the bookstore staff. He snaps a couple of pictures with my camera phone so I can post a picture on my blog tomorrow morning.

Bowing my head, I flip through the pages to the section I wanted to read aloud to this handful of readers—mostly women, mostly white, mostly older than me.

I am reading from the publisher's proof copy—the only one of its kind, the one in which I deleted the acknowledgments to you before you requested through family court mediation that I reinstate the passage, giving you credit for twenty-five years of support. The first excerpt I read is from the chapter about my uncle's sixtieth birthday party, referring to the red eggs in the title, in which my uncle is reborn into wisdom. The second excerpt I read is toward the end of the book when my father comes home from the hospital and I express my desire to become a professional artist. In that scene I confront my father, tell him I'm unhappy living the life he wants me to live, and for the first time since I wrote those words I feel like I am reliving those moments again with you. Instead of confronting my father, of disobeying him and challenging him to acknowledge I want a different life, I am breaking free of you, cart wheeling into a life of my own.

When I finish reading, I glance up at the audience. A few people raise their hands. They ask questions I cannot answer—questions I never anticipated.

"Do you still paint?" an elderly woman asks.

"I do, but not for a living anymore." I blink, fighting back the emotions rising in my chest. I gave up my art business after a loan officer scoffed at my business plan.

How many hours do you intend to devote to this enterprise? he asked.

Ten hours a week, I said.

That's not enough for a two hundred fifty thousand dollar loan. You need to invest at least twice that amount or hire a part-time employee.

I can't afford more time. But with the money from the loan, I will hire an employee.

At the time, you were developing your own computer repair business. I was working a corporate job with a dependable salary and health benefits. If we didn't have a family, especially a child with special needs, I could have been selfish and chosen differently. But when the loan officer insisted I quit my job and devote all of my time licensing my artwork, I was honest and told him I couldn't, which resulted in my loan being declined. Since I couldn't fulfill my obligations to outstanding clients and vendors, I closed my art business, canceling my dreams rather than delaying them, and focused on my remaining passion—writing.

After I sign copies of my book, I meet with the

Knight of Cups and the bookstore staff by the cash register.

"Is she always this poised?" the sales clerk asks the Knight of Cups.

He blushes and stammers. He has never witnessed my public persona other than one book signing at a local mom-and-pop store where he bought a copy of my short stories two years ago.

A sharp pang clutches my chest. You would have answered that question with ease. *She's a lot better than she was when she started. At her first reading, she had troubles adjusting the microphone and no one could hear her. At her second reading, she rushed through the words and no one comprehended what she had read. At her third reading, she finally discovered a cadence. Our daughter calls it 'Mommy's reading voice' but I call it pure magic.*

The sales clerk presses. "You've been with her for twenty-five years, surely you have an impression."

The Knight of Cups looks lost. I touch his elbow and smile trying to smooth over the sudden awkwardness without getting too personal. "He's never been to one of these readings."

The sales clerk flips to the back of the book and runs a finger down the last page of the acknowledgments. "But you said he's accepted awards on your behalf."

She thinks the Knight of Cups is you. But you are three thousand miles away cooking dinner for our children. I heave a sigh. If you were here, you would tell her your favorite story about the time I won a local writing competition. Since I was attending a writer's retreat in Vermont, I could not attend the event and accept the check for several hundred dollars. Even after the sitter canceled, you drove across town and stood with our children on stage to read my award-winning story and accept the prize money. The audience gave you a standing ovation. You even signed copies of the published story with your name followed by "the Poet's Husband" after your favorite Molly Giles' short story. The local paper wrote about the event, and you sent me a copy. Even the reporter referred to you as "the Poet's Husband." But you'll always be my Magician, casting your spells and creating your illusions, dazzling the world with your presence.

I could use some of your magic right now.

"That paragraph refers to another man." I swallow. Hot shame fills me. "My soon-to-be ex-husband." I wave toward the Knight of Cups. "This is my boyfriend. We've been dating for six months."

Eyebrows raise. Mouths open. Silence ensues.

The sales clerk shoves a stack of books for me to sign for the display rack and offers me a bar of locally made chocolate as a thank you gift for my time.

Standing outside in the aftermath of rain, waiting for another taxi to take us to the hotel in Arlington, I feel the alienation bleeding from my personal life into my professional life, and wonder if anyone else has ever felt this way. The judgment I have for my father in the book parallels the judgment I feel from these strangers who were looking for someone they expected to find only to discover she had been replaced by someone else.

The ride to the hotel is full of pregnant silence.

After checking into our room, we wander down to the hotel's restaurant and bar.

The hostess leads us to the outdoor balcony seating beneath a clear sky full of stars. The scent of jasmine from the planters along the perimeter of the building settles like a thick coat of perfume.

The Knight of Cups orders a double vodka martini and chicken wings.

I order hot chamomile tea and a salad.

"No cocktail tonight?" He raises his glass in a toast.

I shake my head and click my mug to his glass. "Cheers."

The hot tea burns my tongue. The air smells damp from the recent rains. Heat lamps break up the chill. The atmosphere is warm and romantic— the perfect setting for a couple newly in love.

My cell phone pings. I remove the phone from my purse and swipe the screen.

—*Did you make it on time to the reading?*—

Your concern both comforts and disturbs me. I twist my lips in a grimace and type.

—*Yes, but everyone asked about you. They had questions only the Poet's Husband could answer.*—

Seconds tick by before my phone pings with a response.

—*Did you tell them about our divorce?*—

My throat constricts. I glance up to catch the Knight of Cups' expression, but he has shifted on the chair to catch the last minutes of the first game of the World Series. I bow my head and type.

—*Not in those words, but yes.*—

Even though we have not finalized our divorce

and are nowhere near an agreement on most things, we are headed in that direction.

Resignation settles against my shoulders. I heave a sigh and turn off my phone.

The Knight of Cups cheers. "Kansas City won." He lifts his empty glass to the server. "Another double, please."

When I catch his triumphant gaze, I force a smile. I finish the limp and tasteless salad and sip the dregs of the now lukewarm, flowery tea. At least tomorrow, I have a reprieve from public torture.

The Knight of Cups has booked us a duck tour on a retired military vehicle that can travel on both land and sea.

I don't care about the sightseeing.

I only care I do not have to be picture perfect for anyone.

I can be a tourist, invisible and anonymous.

A shadow next to him.

A memory next to you.

∼

IN THE MORNING, MY PHONE TRILLS. BLINKING IN the filmy light filtering in through the closed curtains, I roll over in the huge, downy, king-sized hotel bed and unhook my phone from the charger on the night stand. A quick glance informs me the call is from my publicist. Sitting against the plush pillows, I swipe the screen.

"Can you make it to a TV studio in Chicago for a live interview tomorrow morning at seven?"

Her breathless voice washes over me. Standing,

I rifle through my backpack for the flight itinerary.

The Knight of Cups rolls over, folding a pillow over his head, trying to fall back to sleep.

"My flight to Chicago leaves Dulles at that time." Disappointment sags against my chest. Why didn't I have my publicist book the flights in addition to booking the engagements?

"Don't worry. We can work toward a solution."

Her voice assumes a take-charge battle cry.

"Can you switch your flight to today? That will give you time to settle and have a good night's sleep. The TV studio can send a car to your hotel at six. You need to be in the green room for wardrobe and makeup by six-thirty. You'll have a fifteen minute slot starting at seven."

I run my fingers through my knotted hair. "Give me twenty minutes, and I'll call you back."

"What's wrong?" The Knight of Cups hugs the pillow and squints.

"My publicist secured a spot on TV." I grab my laptop and turn it on. "I need to get to Chicago today for an appearance tomorrow morning."

"Here. Let me help you." He scrambles out of bed, slipping on a T-shirt and shorts, before taking over the laptop. He scans the listings and points. "The only direct flight leaves today at noon."

"How much?" I remove my credit card from my wallet. We will have to cancel the duck tour of Washington D.C.

He types for a moment before he stops and frowns. "Seven hundred dollars."

"Total?"

"Each."

I gasp, dropping the credit card on the desk. No publisher is fronting the bill for this nation-wide book tour. I secured just enough speaking engagements to break even on this trip. Seven hundred dollars will have to come out of the marital funds that are tied up in family court. Even if I charge the expense on my personal credit card, I will have to get your written permission to pay it.

He drums his fingers on the table and gazes at our reflections in the mirror. "I don't want to cancel our sightseeing trip. I've never been to the capital. It's the only thing I've been looking forward to since you said I could come along."

Gaping, I throw up my arms. "But it's a TV appearance."

He shrugs. "Nobody who sees you on TV is coming to the book signing to buy your book."

"How do you know?" I pace across the thin carpet in my bare feet, thinking you would gladly cancel a sightseeing trip anywhere in the world for the opportunity of a fifteen minute TV interview. But you're not here. You're either asleep or in the kitchen feeding Forever Child a middle of the night snack. "Oprah's Book Club sold millions of books for authors."

"You're not being interviewed by Oprah." He stands and yawns. "Your slot is what time?"

"Seven."

"Everyone is getting ready for work. No one is thinking about books. They're only tuning in for the weather."

I slip into the vacated chair and study the computer screen. "You can keep your flight for tomorrow and meet me at the bookstore. I'll change my flight for the TV appearance."

"What?" He slumps against the edge of the mattress. "Why would you do that? I don't want to travel alone."

I study his reflection in the mirror. He looks like a selfish child rubbing his face with his hands. A heat of fury sweeps over me. Isn't this the same man who offered to pay for my trip to New York City to attend the Book Expo earlier this year? I chose not to go, anchored to my family. Now, as a free, unencumbered woman, I swivel to face him. "This trip is business." I point to the carpet. "*You* can stay for pleasure. *I* need to conduct business." Turning, I reach for the credit card.

"No." He intercepts me, snatching the credit card. "Please, stay."

Frowning, I drum my fingers on the desk. "Give me one reason."

He drops to his knees. "I can't make memories with you if you're not here with me."

"I can't sell books if I stay." I hold his pleading gaze.

Standing, he tosses the credit card on the desk. "You asked me for one reason, and I gave it to you. Isn't that enough?" He throws open his arms. "What more do you want from me?"

"To grow up." I lurch to my feet and thrust my hand out, tucking a finger toward the palm as I count. "First, you asked me to leave my marriage to be with you. Second, you asked me to give up my children and move in with you. Third, you asked me to stay and sightsee with you. What's the next thing you'll ask me to give up?"

"If you're so damned concerned about selling books, I'll buy a thousand copies and donate them to literacy programs." A vein throbs in his temple.

I pace toward the window and pull back the curtain. The sky is bunched up with clouds as tight as angry fists. "It's a horrible day to go sightseeing."

"Why do you care?" He spits out the words. "You aren't staying." He grabs my clothes from the drawers and tosses them into the gaping mouth of my suitcase. "Have a safe trip."

Panic rushes through my arms and legs and jump starts my heartbeat. "Are you breaking up with me?"

He shrugs. "We want different things."

Another flare of anger shoots through me. "I just want to go to the interview."

"Then go." He steps aside and waves to the packed suitcase. "I'm not stopping you."

I heave a sigh. "Why won't you come with me?"

His silence speaks for him.

For a long moment, I think about what I'm losing—a man who loves me, who dines with me, who comes to bed with me and wakes up with me, who wants to make memories with me—against what I'm gaining—an interview on live TV. Is one worth more than the other? I glance at the length of his naked body, and a warm feeling washes over me. He is a selfish man but I love him anyway. After rushing over to him, I place a hand on his arm. "I'll stay."

He meets my gaze. "Are you sure? I don't want you to hold this decision against me."

I nod. I am my father's daughter. But unlike my

father, I don't gamble with money. I gamble with my heart.

He opens his arms and embraces me.

The burst of affection buoys me. "What do I tell my publicist?"

"Tell her, you can't change your flight." Smiling, he pecks my lips one last time before hopping into the shower.

While listening to the plunk of water through the pipes in the wall, I perch on the edge of the mattress and call back my publicist to decline the TV interview.

"Are you sure?" she asks.

I hear the hesitancy in her voice. "Yes, I'm sure."

∿

A COUPLE OF HOURS LATER, THE KNIGHT OF CUPS and I take a taxi to Washington D.C.

After a brief ride, the driver pulls up along the curb of Union Station.

The Knight of Cups holds the door open for me.

I step from the warm cab into the gray, watery light. Already a drizzle blankets my shoulders.

Holding hands, we scuttle into the marble building searching for the ticket booth where we can claim our reservations for the ten-thirty duck tour.

At a glass encased office, an African American woman hands us our tickets, two yellow rain slickers, and two duck whistles. "It gets really wet out there."

I don the yellow rain slicker.

"You look like a giant lemon," the Knight of Cups says. "Stay here. I'm going to find out where we're supposed to meet, and then I'll come back for you." He stalks into the crowd and disappears.

While I'm waiting, I decide to use the bathroom one more time. By the time I return, I see him frowning, calling my name, waving his arms.

A look of panic strikes his face. I rush through the crowd, dodging elbows and purses. "I'm here!"

When he finally glimpses me, he breaks into a smile and opens his arms. "I found my giant lemon!"

His embrace is all encompassing.

I have never been held so tightly, not by you and not by our children and not by anyone else I've ever known.

When he finally releases me, he grips my shoulders. His blue eyes sparkle. "I was afraid I'd lost you." He shakes his head and trips on his voice. "I never—want—to lose—you." He folds me to his chest and sobs. I rub his back and wonder how many people he has lost.

Holding my hand, he guides me to the duck boat on the other side of the building.

We sit side by side on a bench amidst other tourists from all over the country and all over the world.

Our captain steers us through the city, pointing out the sites, from the White House to the Smithsonian and everything in between.

Rain pelts against the yellow slicker and mists my glasses until I can barely see.

Every now and then, he tightens his arm

around my shoulders and kisses my temple and whispers, "I love my giant lemon."

After touring the streets, the duck boat dips into the Potomac River and glides past the Pentagon. The captain cuts the engine and allows the amphibious vehicle to float like a buoy along the current. Planes fly overhead from Reagan Airport. The rain continues to pour. By the time we arrive back at Union Station, we are both drenched.

We decide to skip the bus tour and head to the air museum to dry off.

After two hours of examining objects surrounding the history of air planes, from Kitty Hawk to 747's, we decide to walk around the city and take in as many monuments as we can before it gets dark. Beneath a constant drizzle, we walk ten miles stopping at the Jefferson Memorial, the Lincoln Memorial, the Washington Memorial, the Franklin Delano Roosevelt Memorial, the Vietnam Veterans Memorial, the Martin Luther King, Jr. Memorial, the Korean War Veterans Memorial, and the World War II Memorial. On our way back to Arlington, we cross the bridge with the Seabees Memorial (the Knight of Cups' father was a Seabee), stride past the Arlington Cemetery, and pause at the Iwo Jima Memorial before climbing the steep ascent to the hotel. My throat is dry, having drank only from water fountains at each memorial, and my stomach is growling from skipping lunch. The flimsy yellow slicker dangles from my shoulders like limp banana peels. My feet ache, and my pants cling to my thighs from the persistent rainfall.

"You're a trooper." Smiling, he wraps an arm around my shoulders. "You're not like most women who wilt in the rain." He squeezes my shoulder. "You're tough. Like my mother."

The compliment collides with thoughts about the missed TV appearance. I decide to brush aside all worries. We may have dated for only six months and lived together for only two months but after today we have over 200 years of history between us.

~

THAT NIGHT, I DON'T TEXT YOU ABOUT THE National Mall and Memorial Parks in Washington D.C. I don't mention the National Air and Space Museum, the duck tour, or how the Pentagon is like a little city with its own doctors, grocery stores, and dry cleaners. I don't give you the itinerary for tomorrow: one reading at Boswell Bookstore, first stop at Chicago, Illinois, with a two hour layover before arriving in Milwaukee, Wisconsin. I don't tell you about my fears of another delay, and how I hope that does not happen since I am having dinner with a loyal reader who helped secure the venue.

But as I lie awake next to the Knight of Cups who is already sleeping, I think about texting you. I want to know what you're doing, how you and the children have been, if anyone misses me as much as I miss them.

After turning the phone over and over in my hands, I plug it into the charger on the night stand, fluff the pillows, and curl onto my side facing the

Knight of Cups. The gentle rise and fall of his breathing tugs the sheet against my shoulder. In spite of the physical exertion of walking over ten miles, I am awake, alert, and alone.

I don't belong to you anymore.

I am a satellite spinning out of orbit.

Can I navigate my life alone?

Or does this man lying beside me have the gravitational pull to keep me in his galaxy?

~

"YOU'RE HERE." THE BLONDE JUMPS UP FROM HER seat at the back of the Mexican restaurant. "We finally meet." She wraps her arms around my back and holds me close like we are reunited sisters.

Sydney smiles when she releases me. She looks just like her photographs on social media—medium height and build, mid-thirties, with dirty blond hair and brown eyes and a thousand watt smile. We met online when I released my first novel, *Legs*. For the past seven years, she has been a loyal reader, following my blog, reading my paranormal romance and short story collection, and now arranging with my publicist the reading at Boswell Bookstore.

I briefly introduce her to the Knight of Cups who shakes her hand.

After taking a seat at the loud, noisy table toward the back of the busy restaurant, we browse the menu and chat.

"I passed up an opportunity to appear on the local TV show this morning," I say, twisting the napkin in my lap.

The Knight of Cups reaches underneath the table to hold my hand, calming my clawing fingers. "We stayed to tour Washington D.C. in the rain. We walked over ten miles, taking in all the outdoor monuments." He squeezes my hand and smiles. "Best day of my life."

I lean closer to her and ask, "I'm just afraid I missed an opportunity to sell more books."

"Which TV station?" She sips on her margarita.

I rattle off the major network-affiliated station.

She scrunches her nose and shakes her head. "No one watches that program." She tips back her head and laughs. "I worked there for five years. We were always trying to book important people for interviews, but everyone always went with our competitor. You didn't miss anything."

Exhaling with relief, I glimpse a wide smile on the Knight of Cups.

After dinner, the three of us stroll down the street to Boswell Book Company. The air is crisp and chill and dry like champagne.

At the entrance, a flyer advertising the reading is plastered to the door.

"Stand there, and let me take a picture," the Knight of Cup says.

I stand beside my photograph and smile. I am wearing a teal blouse and the new, fluffy white sweater and the gray, wool slacks from the first night. An accent necklace of turquoise and diamonds, which the Knight of Cups won in a silent auction at another charity event, graces my neckline.

Inside, the bookstore sprawls like a cozy mansion full of rows and rows of colorful books.

The event manager, a jovial man, leads us to the back of the store where a plush reading chair and two sofas are arranged in a circle. "If too many people show up, we'll move you to the other side of the store with the podium and fold out chairs."

But, like the first night, only a handful of readers show up.

We sit on the sofas and chairs like a book club in someone's living room, taking turns sharing stories about our childhoods. I don't read the planned excerpts, preferring to dip into the book and extract whatever scene is appropriate for the flow of conversation.

I sign books for the last fifteen minutes.

Sydney buys several copies for family and friends. I personalize the autographs for each one, asking for the correct spelling of each recipient's name. A few readers who arrived late or who wandered over from browsing the aisles also stand in line. By the end of the evening, I've sold twice as many books as the first night.

The event manager waves me to the store room and allows me to select one of the advanced reader copies the bookstore receives for preorders. I scan the titles and locate one written by a writer I know: *Up from the Sea* by Leza Lowitz. Feeling generous, I also purchase a copy of Billy Collins poetry, which I intend to read to my son, who has graduated from listening to Dr. Seuss to something more sophisticated.

Light and buoyant from the conversation, the book signing, and the new treasures, I leave the bookstore and follow the Knight of Cups to our rental car parked across the street. I hug Sydney goodbye one last time and thank her again for all of her support.

The sky is dark and clear. The air is still crisp and cool and dry.

That night, tucked beneath the scratchy covers of the hotel bed, I drift to sleep without worries. For once, my reckless gambling paid off. I didn't miss the once-in-a-lifetime opportunity of reaching thousands of viewers on a local TV station. I bonded with Knight of Cups instead.

~

THE NEXT MORNING, I WAKE AT SIX, SHOWER, change, and pack. With a large coffee and a fast food breakfast sandwich, I sit in the passenger seat of the rental car. The Knight of Cups is driving the two and a half hour trip to Tomah, Wisconsin, where I am scheduled to read at the local middle and high schools, starting at ten-thirty.

Although I am a morning person, I am grateful for him driving. The roads are a little slick from a dusting of early snow. I have never driven in inclement weather, but he has. His parents owned a condo in Lake Tahoe, and he would travel there every winter to ski with his friends from college.

The ride is full of silence while we listen to snippets of comedy acts on satellite radio.

"My brother a professional comedian." He drums his fingers against the steering wheel. "He changed his name and performs all over the country."

"What's his stage name?"

He smiles and shakes his head. "I'll let him tell

you that. He usually doesn't like friends or family members watching him perform."

I fiddle with the edge of my black wool coat. "I understand. Talking in front of a roomful of strangers is much easier than trying to entertain a handful of family or friends."

We arrive in Tomah an hour ahead of my first presentation and meet up with Amanda, the teacher who has coordinated the day's events. Months ago, I reached out to Amanda after reading an article she wrote about writing, and we have kept in touch ever since. My book, which is perfect for middle grade readers, became the book of the month for the school. Strolling through the wide halls, glimpsing students carrying dog-eared copies of my book in their arms, I feel a swell of pride like I am a sudden celebrity.

In the tight stall of the girls' bathroom, I change into my red, silk cheongsam and black heels. I leave my hair down, my glasses on, and grab my copy of my book. Handing my backpack to the Knight of Cups, I follow Amanda into the quiet of the school's library where a space has been carved out for me to give my presentation about resilience.

The bell rings, and students file into the room. By the time the presentation begins, I guess I have about two hundred students from several grades sitting cross-legged on the carpeted floor. I have never performed for such a big group of strangers, and I feel my knees wobble and my throat constrict. I suddenly wish I had brought a thermos full of water.

But after Amanda's sweet introduction, I begin.

I share with the students snippets from my life growing up Chinese American before the advent of multiculturalism. I read the same two excerpts I read the first night, and I field questions. So many questions. The hands shoot up and wave like thigh-high weeds in a field of clover. I pick as many students as I can and answer their concerns as best as I can with the amount of time I have.

The line for the book signing is long.

I sign personalized autographs for each student.

Before the next round of students arrives, Amanda introduces me to a reporter from the local paper who interviews me about the book and my life.

The tall, wiry man with gray hair pushes the glasses up the bridge of his nose and removes a pen from the breast pocket of his plaid shirt. He licks the tip of the pen when the ink refuses to move over the page of his notebook.

At first, the questions are benign—who are your favorite authors, what inspired you—but then the conversation quickly pivots.

"Are you a full-time artist like the girl in the book wanted to be?"

Again I feel that punch to the gut moment like I felt that first night. Do I want to share that story —the one where I chose my family over my ambition even after I sacrificed that family to be here? Or do I keep a veil of privacy? I squirm, shifting my weight from foot to foot before I respond. "Not anymore."

He leans forward, eyebrows raised, pen poised. "What do you do to make a living?"

"I work for a community bank."

"Ah-ha! Your father was right." He steps back and scrawls something on his notepad. "You can't make a living following your passion." He narrows his gaze. "Why did you deceive those students by telling them to follow their dreams even though you're not living them?"

Heat and shame inflame my face. My whole body trembles. I glance at Amanda, talking with the Knight of Cups, and the librarian who is ushering the next group of students into the room, and realize I am alone.

Suddenly, I wish you were here. You would know how to respond to this stranger. You would challenge his assumption that I am misguiding these students into believing in themselves when I should be preaching about abandoning their hearts' desires and entering practical professions just as my father preached to me when I was their age. But you are not here to defend me or my work. You are over 2,000 miles away making our children breakfast.

I inhale deeply and release the breath slowly and uncurl my fists. "I went to college with so many people who said they were going to be artists and they were going to writers, but they don't write or paint, even in their free time. To be a painter, you need to paint. To be a writer, you need to write. Professional success is a bonus." Tears well up in my eyes, and I feel like that little girl again, the one I wrote about in that book, the one I thought I had finally released. "You need to keep that faith in yourself, because the world will beat it out of you if it can."

The interview ends.

For the rest of the afternoon, I shift my focus to the students, even the high school students who don't care about the book or the presentation or the extra credit they are receiving for attending the event.

The next day, before leaving Tomah for the drive back to Milwaukee, I pick up the local paper. My photograph graces the front page with the title, "Triumph of Identity." But the article is anything but triumphant. First, I find all the errors —I attended Northwestern *before* graduating from high school but the reporter wrote that I attended *after*, I wrote for the local paper *before* earning my bachelor's degree but the reporter wrote that I worked there *after*. As a former journalist, I am incensed by the lack of fact checking. But what stings most of all is I am referred to by my old name, which is yours. In mediation, you asked me to take back my maiden name, which I have as evidenced by the book cover, but this reporter doesn't know about the court order in our divorce proceedings and has not bothered to dig deep enough to discover this public information. He has not even bothered to reference the book cover. Did he even study journalism?

"What's wrong?" The Knight of Cups is driving through another light dusting of snow.

I rub my forehead, forgetting I have just touched newsprint, and staunch the overwhelming feelings rising inside. "The article is inaccurate." I heave a sigh. "I come across as someone else."

"No, you don't." He skimmed the article in the

hotel room while I was packing. "You come across just fine."

I shudder, thinking, *He doesn't know me*. Six months since we started dating, and he thinks of me as someone else.

After a glance over his shoulder, he passes a slower vehicle on the two lane freeway. "I just wish they would have printed the photograph with you signing the books for the kids."

I shake my head. "They would have needed written permission from their parents to use their likeness in print because they are minors." The business of publishing never leaves me.

Frowning, he swipes a sidelong glance in my direction. "What else is wrong?"

I am not a full-time artist. I work in a community bank. I write early in the mornings and every other weekend. I am just like everyone else working a practical job. The only difference is I haven't given up on this second dream of writing even if I gave up on my first love of art. I bow my head and stare at my feet. "I come across as a failure in the article."

"You're not a failure." He reaches over and squeezes my cold, newsprint-smeared hand.

I meet his kind gaze.

"You're my giant lemon." He winks and smiles. "I love my giant lemon."

I giggle.

But deep inside, I worry if I have steered these unsuspecting students into a harder life, a life full of creativity and disappointment, much like my own.

~

By the time I return to California, I am exhausted.

I cancel a promotional opportunity at Book Passages in Corte Madera, but keep my commitment to Green Apple Books in San Francisco only because your sister has promised to attend.

I cross the Golden Gate Bridge into San Francisco and find parking. I'm two hours early for the event. Wandering up and down the sloping streets, I stop at a Chinese store and a bakery to purchase chops sticks and moon cakes, respectively. After dropping those items off in the trunk of my old four-door sedan, I march over to the Catholic Church and kneel in the pews before the statues of the Virgin Mary and the Sacred Heart of Jesus and pray. Afterward, I stroll two doors down from the bookstore and eat an early sushi dinner.

By the time the sun has set, I arrive at the bookstore. The space is small, narrow, and crammed with second hand books that smell like mildew. I follow the clerk up to the third floor where an old leather chair is setup against the window and pillows have been thrown down on the floor for the audience to sit.

My publicist blusters up the stairs and throws her arms around my neck. "So good to finally meet," she says, all teeth and shining eyes. She takes a few strategic photographs with me in the leather chair signing extra copies for the bookstore and promises to send out more press releases to capture any interest now that the official tour is winding toward an end.

A few minutes after I begin reading, your sister arrives. She has cut her red hair shorter than the last time I've seen her in April when she came for a day-long visit while you were still in Arizona. Tonight she is alone. Her husband and her elementary school-aged daughter are home in San Jose. She finds a seat on a velvet cushion and listens.

I smile wider when I see her.

Afterward, she stays behind until I've signed the last book for the last customer, an elderly Chinese American woman who is also writing her memoirs about growing up in the Bay Area.

"I'm hungry," your sister says.

I suggest the Japanese restaurant where I already ate, and we step inside and sit at the bar. The lights are low, the music is soft, and the ambiance is as fluid as the fish swimming in the tanks behind the bartender. I drink some hot tea while your sister eats California rolls and sips water.

She is the only member of your family who still acknowledges my presence.

"You look good," she says, glancing up and down the length of my body. "Divorce does you good, girl."

I smirk and murmur about the thirty pounds I have gained since dating the Knight of Cups.

"You were too skinny when you were with my brother," she says. "I could see your collar bones and your cheek bones. Even your wrists were too bony."

I tell her I miss the hollows on either side of my hips when I lie down.

"Girl, I told you that shits way too skinny. You're healthy now."

Her smile is wide and generous. When she reaches over to hug me, I smell the sad, sweet fragrance of her perfume that brings back countless memories of the holidays we've shared as family.

Are we family anymore?

Toward the end of the meal, she points with her chopsticks to my fingers. "Doesn't it feel weird not wearing a ring on your left hand?"

I rub the vacant space that housed the ring you bought me. The tan lines are faded from spending time outside over the summer but not completely gone. "Yes, I feel naked." I don't belong to you anymore. I don't belong to anyone. I am a free woman, but I don't feel free. "I've thought about buying a replacement ring to show my commitment to myself, a one carat emerald cut, which I've always wanted, but can't afford."

"Great idea." Nodding, she chews. "They make affordable Cubic Zirconia rings that look exactly like the real thing. I'm sure you can purchase one for less than one hundred dollars."

I sigh. "I'll have to wait until after the divorce is final. My accounts are frozen until then."

"Well, if I was you, that ring would be my first purchase." She nods and winks.

I laugh.

At the end of dinner, I walk her to her car, which as luck would have it, is parked next to mine. I hold her tightly, thinking about all things I have not told her: my regrets about leaving you, my disappointments about choosing my family over my art only to choose another man over my family, and the growing dissatisfaction about who I am becoming—a woman who no longer recognizes herself. I strategically spent the evening focusing on the positives—the sightseeing in Washington D.C., the friends I made in Wisconsin, the relationship I am building with the Knight of Cups.

On the drive home, I turn up the heat and the radio. I know this book tour has been both a welcomed distraction and an awkward bridge between my old life and my new life. In a few days, I will return to work and the family court battles, which don't seem to end.

Only one thing is certain—I am no longer a child battling against her father.

I am an adult woman battling against herself.

~

THE NEXT CARD IN THE DINETTE READING REFERS TO A direction I should take or consider taking. This card is the fork in the road, and I have an opportunity to choose. I draw the High Priestess, a Major Arcana card, which means this fork in the road is not something I ultimately get to decide. Fate has decided for me. I gaze at a woman shaped bottle of secret syrup and laugh. The High Priestess generally means the future is not ours to see, and reading the fine print on her label I discover "the mysteries of the universe are sweeter" than I know. I am stymied by this card I've drawn, which casts a spell trickier than anything you've ever cast. The road I've been advised to take is silent and exists in a realm beyond words or speech. The road I am to take cannot be read. It must be lived. The blueprint has already been sketched on my soul.

~

WITHIN MONTHS, I'VE TRANSFORMED FROM A WIFE and a mother and a career woman to a separated woman living in her boyfriend's house and visiting her children every other weekend at the house she no longer lives in but pays for. Hot shame burns my cheeks and stings the back of my throat. I am no longer a financially independent woman. All of my income is tied in the joint checking account until the mediator we hired can negotiate what's yours and what's mine. For all of my living expenses, I am dependent on the Knight of Cups' generosity.

One evening, despondent over the lack of progress in our divorce proceedings and desperate for relief from the growing guilt over everything I've done to destroy the happiness of our family, I contact my earliest childhood friend, Koon, who I know has suffered a divorce, leaving his first son to be raised with his ex-wife and his former mother-in-law.

He has known me for so long he recognizes my state of mind before I speak. "You're not a bad person. You just feel bad."

I sit on the red leather dining room chair in the Knight of Cups' house with the phone pressed against my ear. I sniffle, twirling a strand a hair at the nape of my neck, a nervous behavior I picked up during elementary school and never shed.

"How did you stop feeling like a failure after your divorce?"

A moment of silence passes between us.

"It took me five years after the divorce to really discover who I am and what I want," he says. "I'm glad my ex-wife was able to raise my son and give him everything I couldn't." He sighs. "For years I only saw him every other holiday. I was busy working, earning my cosmetology degree, and I didn't have a place of my own. After I remarried, when my son was a teenager, he came to live with me and my new wife until he was able to move out on his own." He pauses. "Don't give up. Your boyfriend might change his mind and let you bring your kids over to his house someday. In the meantime, be kind to yourself."

But I can't. I keep referring to myself as a dead-beat mom. I am like the neighbor's ex-husband who used to pull up along the curb every other weekend, honking his horn to alert his son and daughter he was waiting to take them to his new home. "The guy can't even bother to park his car and walk up to the front door," I used to say to you. "What type of man does that?"

Now I know—a man who has forfeited his parental rights.

In mediation, sitting at a long, mahogany table with you and your attorney on one side, I and my attorney on the other, we listen to the mediator at the head of the table inform us of the rules of engagement: no speaking out of turn, no yelling, no name calling, no opinions, only facts.

The facts of the matter boil down to time and

money. How much time am I willing to buy with how much money?

The Knight of Cups wants me to release the children completely, but the mediator reminds me I cannot. "Legally, you must retain minimum contact."

"What does the law define as minimum?" I lace my fingers on the cold table and stare into your eyes.

"That depends on the other party's definition," she says.

You arch your eyebrows. "Right now, she sees them every other weekend at my house."

The mediator pencils out the agreement—around eight percent of custody is mine. You get the other ninety-two percent.

Which also translates into ninety-two percent of my income being paid as temporary spousal and child support until a final agreement can be reached.

When I complain to the Knight of Cups, I am told this is the price of freedom.

But when I lie awake at night, I can't help but think this is the price of a prison I'll never escape.

My attorney agrees. "She'll never afford to buy her own home in this county if she's giving away all of her money."

The mediator shrugs. "If she wants more cash, she'll have to give up more time."

But I can't, so I don't.

At my new residence, I come home from these weekly meetings depleted.

Unable to write, I buy a black canvas the size of a bedroom door and place it on my easel in the dining room and sketch out a painting of a cat in the moon. Over the next few weeks, I paint. I leave the black cat in the naked tree the color of the canvas and swirl a full moon at the center and spiral out the rest of the sky with lavender. When I am finished, I step back from the painting and feel as lonely as the cat in the moon.

The Knight of Cups walks up behind me and wraps his arms around my waist and places his chin on the top of my head. "That cat reminds me of your daughter."

"Why?"

He kisses the top of my head. "She's has her back to us. She's alone. The moon is full and the night is all around her." He releases me. "Maybe you should give that painting to her for Christmas."

"She's not talking to me." Although you have bought her a cell phone, she does not respond to my text messages or voicemails. "She wrote me a Dear John letter about how she never wants to see me again. I've broken up her family. I've stolen what love was left for us."

He heaves a sigh and touches my shoulder. "Don't give up."

But I do.

I hang the Cat in the Moon in the music room against the wall. No one can see it unless they are walking from one end of the house to the other. At night, in the shadowy lights of the kitchen, the whole painting glows with an eerie incandescence as if the moon truly is captured in the room.

By the time the holiday season barrels closer,

you offer an olive branch—I can see our daughter the day after Thanksgiving.

I make reservations for us at Cattlemen's and pick her up at your home. She is dressed in a sweater and pants, her long, brown hair flowing freely down her back. She slides into the passenger seat and straps the seatbelt across her lap. She is cold and silent like you when we fight. I tap away at her resistance, asking about school, her friends, her life since I left the family. With one word responses, she slowly crumples. By the time we are seated in the full restaurant, she confesses she wrote and sent the Dear John letter at the insistence of the counselor you both are seeing.

Pain seizes beneath my breastbone. I can't dwell on the ache, so I shift my focus to the beautiful young woman beside me who has your freckled cheeks and sense of humor and my dark hair and almond shaped eyes.

Our server, a young man attending the local college, takes our picture for us.

I send the picture to the Knight of Cups.

He responds with a smiley face.

While we are eating—salmon for me, steak for our daughter—the Knight of Cups' mother and brother stop by our table to say hello since they have been dining at the same restaurant when they received the Knight of Cups' news of our presence.

Our daughter smiles and shakes hands. When they leave, she turns to me and says, "They're nice."

Hope blooms in my chest.

Before I take her back home, she asks to see where I live. She says she is curious.

I drive her the two miles to the home I share with the Knight of Cups and unlock the front door. No one is home. The Knight of Cups and his dog have left to visit his mother and brother at his mother's house.

Our daughter pads through the great room, which combines the dining room, living room, and kitchen, and into the music room. She stops and stares at the Cat in the Moon. "Did you paint that?"

"Yes, I did…for you. I was going to give it to you for Christmas."

She smiles and clasps her hands to her chest. "Lavender is my favorite color."

"Yes, I know." I mirror her smile.

Next, she walks across the family room with the built-in bookshelves and steps into the office and the master bedroom. She asks if she can use the restroom. I point her down the hall. When she emerges minutes later, she steps on the vents blowing up heat from the floor. "What's that?" she asks.

"We have forced air heating at this house."

She takes off her shoes and places her sock-covered feet on the grate and wiggles her toes. "I like this house," she says. "Where would I stay if I visited you?"

I take her small, warm hand in my larger, cooler hand and lead her back across the house to the children's bedrooms. The first room facing the street is smaller with a queen-sized mattress and scraggly curtains. "His son stays here when he visits."

The next bedroom is larger with two twin beds and a nightstand. The walls are painted lavender and the curtains match. "Who stays in this room?" she asks.

"His daughters."

"Where would I stay?" She glances at me, an eyebrow arched.

I shrug. "Which room would you want to stay in?" I don't anticipate a visit ever happening, not with the current status of our negotiations, but I am the Fool—I live off daydreams, wishes, and prayers. With faith, I know nothing is impossible.

She runs her gaze across the lavender walls. "I'd stay in this room." She turns and smiles, filling me with hope.

By the time I return her to the martial home, I feel something has sprouted between us, a seedling of some sort I can't define.

She hugs me one last time, and you open the door and swallow her inside.

I thank you for the gift of seeing her tonight.

You nod and close the door.

When I return home, the Knight of Cups and his dog are back. "How did the evening go?"

"Wonderful," I say. "We had a three hour dinner then I brought her here because she wanted to see where I lived."

"You brought her here?"

The rise of his voice startles me. Should I have asked permission? "I'm sorry. I thought it would be okay."

He stands beside the kitchen island and sips his

drink. "Sure, I guess." He narrows his gaze for a long moment before lifting his chin. "What did she think?"

"She seemed to like the house." I shift my weight from foot to foot. "She asked where she would stay if she visited."

With a long arm, he waves toward the bedrooms. "Either room. Doesn't matter. My kids are hardly here anymore."

His youngest daughter stayed with us for a week after I moved in. But she hasn't been back since.

"She liked the girls' room. The walls are painted her favorite color."

He points toward the music room. "Did she see your painting?"

I nod.

"And?" He places his hands against his hips. "What did she think?"

"She liked it."

He smiles. "I knew she would."

A month passes. I thought the divorce would be finalized. Agreements have been made on most issues—from child custody and payments to the division of the house and debts. But between the holiday schedules of the attorneys, the mediator, and the courts, the divorce won't be finalized until after the start of the New Year. In the meantime, you agree I can drop off our children's presents and visit for a few hours the day after Christmas.

You invite me inside and ask if I will stay for a movie. Why not? I sink onto the black leather sofa beside the Christmas tree decorated with the ornaments we've collected over the years, some dating back to our childhood. I sniff and pretend my allergies are acting up. I don't want you to know I miss spending the holidays with you and our families. I don't want you to know I miss this life I left.

But you don't seem to notice. You play Jim Carrey's version of *Dr. Seuss' How the Grinch Stole Christmas*, and we sit side by side and laugh. We have seen this movie before, but this time holds a special poignancy. Our divorce has hardened our hearts like the Grinch, but our children have softened them like Cindy Lou Who.

Forever Child wanders into and out of the room. We press Pause to the movie to address his needs—a diaper change, a meal, a request for music—and spend the next three hours playing at being a family again.

By the end of the movie, a magic spell has woven over us. You stretch your arm along the back of the leather sofa, and I rest my head against your shoulder. You trace circles on my upper arm with the pads of your fingers, and I close my eyes and breathe in the heady scent of your woodsy cologne.

Our daughter walks into the room and stops to stare. "Are you guys getting back together?"

I lift my head and blink my eyes.

You remove your arm from the back of the sofa.

The spell is broken.

A gulf opens up between us.

Wide-eyed, she lingers on the cusp of the doorway.

I don't know what she's thinking. The

knocking of my blood ticks against my skin. I'm too afraid to ask.

"Do you like your gift?" I shift my hips on the sofa, and the springs squeak against my weight. I brought the Cat in the Moon painting for her.

She nods. "I already hung it in my room. Want to see?"

I stroll down the narrow hallway and step into the cotton-candy room. Above her bed, which is pressed against one wall, hangs the Cat in the Moon. I bend down and kiss her forehead. "I'm glad you like it. It looks good in here."

Tilting her head to the side, she looks at me. "Are you and Dad getting back together?"

"Do you want us to?" The divorce is almost final. Why would I want to go back? Why would you? But the possibility opens. Should I discuss this turn-of-events with you? I sigh, thinking of your arm stretched behind the sofa, my head on your shoulder, and the incredible peace between us. Were we just pretending to be a happy family again or was the feeling real?

Shrugging, she bites her lower lip and stammers, "I—don't—know."

She looks as conflicted as I feel.

"It's okay not to know." I open my arms.

After stepping into my embrace, she holds me for a long moment.

I glance up at the Cat in the Moon. The solitary creature hangs suspended against the wall, a sentinel in this domestic war. The power of the moon's intuition and the confusion of the swirls of light mirror the space inside what was once our family. A sense of comfort and security rises up within me. Even if our daughter is here without me, she isn't alone anymore.

～

THE NEXT CARD CONTAINS THE HEART OF THE MATTER, the crux of the dilemma, the story beneath the story. This is a significant event, one that could change every-thing. I turn over the card. The Seven of Swords is reversed. Three female friends gossip around a platter of five knives. Another woman smiles behind them, wielding two knives in her hands. Back stabbing bitches, *I think, but the card is reversed. In tarot read-ings, reversals signify either the opposite meaning of the card or energy that is stuck and unyielding. Thus, the Seven of Swords, which would ordinarily mean lies and deception, is tossed upside down in a reversal—all lies and deception will end, and the truth will finally be revealed.*

～

ON THE MORNING I AM TO MEET WITH THE mediator to sign the final divorce decree, I hear my phone ring where I left it on the dining room table.

I am on the other side of the house, brushing my teeth. I spit and rinse, drying my mouth with a blue face towel as I stride across several rooms. The phone stops ringing as soon as I cross the threshold but within a few moments starts again.

I glance at an unknown number and swipe the screen. "Hello?"

"Is this Princess Pea's mom?"

The woman's voice is pert and formal. I wonder if she's a teacher or a school nurse. The hour is early enough for either of them to call. "Yes? Is she all right?"

"No, she isn't."

The bottom falls from my stomach, and I pull back a red chair from the dining room table and sit. A list of potential problems flits through my mind. *Has she fallen sick at school? Is someone bullying her again? Has she not been turning in her homework?* I wet my lips. "What happened?"

"She's been hurting herself."

"Hurting herself?"

"She's been cutting the inside of her thighs with a razor," the woman explains. "She says she'll commit suicide unless she can move out of her father's home immediately."

"Immediately?"

The Knight of Cups strides into the room and touches my shoulder.

I mouth the words "Princess Pea" and point to the phone.

"I'm the counselor she and her father are seeing in regards to the divorce." She clears her throat and continues. "I suggest you take her into your home. The other options are I request foster care through family court or I keep her here with me."

"With you?" I suddenly have a case of echolalia.

"Yes, with me."

The Knight of Cups gestures for me to tell him what's going on.

I lower the phone and briefly inform him.

"We'll take her." He points toward the children's bedrooms. "She can stay with us."

"Are you sure?" I narrow my gaze. "I thought you didn't want anything to do with my kids."

"She's in danger of committing suicide." He throws up his arms. "What else can we do?"

What else, indeed.

I lift the phone to my ear. The axis the world has been revolving on suddenly shifts, and everything is tilted toward rather than away. I will have to call the mediator, explain the circumstances, and arrange for another date to negotiate. If she will be living with us, then I will no longer have only eight percent custody. I will have one hundred percent custody of one child and another child every other weekend. My income will no longer be slashed to smithereens. I push back my shoulders. Although I thought the battle was over, I realize the war has not yet been won. "We'll take her."

∾

LATER THAT MORNING, THE KNIGHT OF CUPS AND I arrive in his pickup truck at the marital home. We have both called in sick to work to take care of this family emergency. Rounding the corner of the cul-de-sac, I gasp. All of Princess Pea's belongings have been tossed on the front lawn for the neighbors to see. She huddles beside the Cat in the Moon propped against the bookcase my mother built for me when I was her age. I clench my hands into fists. What have you done?

She rushes over to me, throwing her arms

around my neck, sobbing. "The Empress from Arizona is here." She steps back and rubs her eyes with her fists. "She moved into the house two weeks after you left. Dad said she was only visiting, but she never left. She's been here the whole time, even when you've visited. She was hiding in the master bedroom, being quiet. Dad didn't want you to know she was here. He thought it might ruin the divorce."

I let out a breath and glance at the house. The curtains are open. "Is she here right now?"

She shakes her head. "Dad took her to work with him. That's where she stays when Forever Child and I are at school."

The Knight of Cups releases the tailgate of the truck. "Did you bring your stuff out here?"

"No, Dad did. The counselor called him to let him know you were coming to take me. He was angry, and he threw everything out here. He said I should have kept my mouth shut until tomorrow."

Of course, you did. You didn't want anyone to know about the Empress from Arizona or the daughter who wanted out of your house. You wanted to keep ninety-two percent of my income even while our daughter lived at my boyfriend's house.

Fury burns through my vision, and I sink into the rocking chair near the chain-link fence. Memories of our amicable interactions from watching *The Grinch* to chatting in the mediation room dissolve into a puddle of deception. Any hope of a reunion between us is lost.

During the ride back to the Knight of Cups' house, I learn the rest of the story from our

233

daughter. The Empress has filed for a divorce. She does not want to work. She is hoping the family court will award her alimony for life since she has never been employed during the twenty years she has been married. Oh, and yes, she has asked you for a promise ring. She has chased away your female friends, staking her claim on your heart and your home.

"I was happy at first," our daughter says. "But the Empress became too bossy. She wants to be my mother. I told her I don't need another mother." Our daughter crosses her arms over her chest and glowers. "She went to see her children over the holidays. I thought she was gone forever. When I saw you and Dad sitting together on the couch watching TV, I thought you both might get back together. But the Empress returned. And Dad never mentioned the possibility again."

Suddenly, everything makes sense. That is why you didn't want me to stay and visit when I brought you chicken noodle soup. The Empress was there. That is why you didn't want to get back together with me when I offered to try one more time. She was involved.

As soon as we pull into the driveway, our daughter bounds into the Knight of Cups' house. "I want this room." She points to the girls' room painted lavender. "But I want the bed from this room." She points to the queen-sized mattress in the boy's room.

Within a couple hours, Princess Pea's belongings have been arranged in her new bedroom.

After school, the Knight of Cups' children

come to visit. They want to make Princess Pea feel welcome in her new home.

The Knight of Cups grimaces as squeals of laughter peel through the house.

I remember how he never wanted children.

That night three of the children return to his ex-wife's house.

The rest of us sit at the dining room table eating barbecued chicken, white rice, and mixed vegetables. The dog sits beneath the table, searching for scraps.

In the corner of the room, the news plays on TV.

I glance around the table, bow my head, and say a prayer of thanks for one piece of my life restored.

≈

THE SELF-HARM DOES NOT STOP ONCE OUR daughter moves into the Knight of Cups' house. I am required by court order to attend six months of dialectical behavior therapy (DBT) with Princess Pea or until the referring psychologist is satisfied with our daughter's progress.

Every Thursday afternoon, I leave work early, pick her up from high school, and sit in a semi-circle with other parents and their teenage children who are suffering from a variety of problems —mood disorders, suicidal ideation, self-harm, and substance abuse. The psychologist leading the group meets with us individually once a month. During one session, he reprimands me for destroying our daughter's chances for happiness.

"Divorce destroys lives," he says, curling his fingers around a pen.

I don't ask if he's married or single or divorced. I don't need to know just as I don't need his judgment. I am here for our daughter, for her mental and emotional welfare, and nothing else.

You come to only one appointment.

Forever Child is with the sitter.

You go into the room to speak with the psychologist by yourself, then together with our daughter, and finally with the three of us.

The psychologist taps a pen against a notebook and narrows his gaze. "Your anger," he points to you, "and your drinking," he points to me, "hurt her," he points to Princess Pea. "You all need to deal with the cause underlying your issues if you want your daughter to be healthy again."

You knot your hands into fists. "We've tried marriage counseling."

I nod. "We're both seeing individual counselors."

The psychologist wags his head from side to side. "Then why aren't you calm?" He shakes a finger at you. "And why aren't you sober?" He nods toward me.

Standing, you throw up your arms. "How can I be calm when you're yelling at me?"

I cross my arms over my chest. "I'm not drinking at this present moment." I tap my foot and think of how many hours I have to wait before the Knight of Cups can greet me with a cocktail. "I wouldn't need to escape this situation if you could just help our daughter." I drag my gaze toward our daughter.

Princess Pea cowers in her chair.

The psychologist scribbles something in the notebook then pushes the glasses up the bridge of his nose. "Your daughter won't get well until you both get healthy."

You stride toward the window overlooking the parking lot. "Are you blaming us for her behavior?" You swivel and narrow your gaze.

The psychologist nods.

You throw open your arms. "How am I responsible for her cutting herself?" You thumb your chest. "She doesn't even live with me anymore. How can I control her?"

I nod. "That's right. How can any of us monitor her behavior twenty-four hours a day?" I inhale. "I work full-time. Someone has to pay for health insurance." I exhale. "If she's that bad, can't you lock her up?"

All gazes swivel toward Princess Pea.

She shrinks against the back of the chair and widens her eyes.

After a long moment, the psychologist turns around and taps on the keyboard of his computer. "Your insurance requires a co-pay of six thousand dollars for in-patient behavioral treatment."

I tap my foot. "How much does the full treatment cost?"

The psychologist swivels to face us. "Not more than seventeen thousand dollars."

You whistle soft and low.

"That's more than the cost of the first year of college," I say.

You sit next to our daughter and take her hand in yours. "Do you want to go into inpatient treatment or do you want to go to college? We can't afford both."

She sucks on her bottom lip.

"That's not a decision she should have to make," the psychologist says.

"Fine." You stand and wave a hand toward the medical file. "Commit her today."

Princess Pea lurches to her feet. "No, don't." She glances first at you then at me. "I want to go to college. I promise to stop hurting myself."

The psychologist scoffs. "You can't just stop hurting yourself. You need professional treatment."

"I'm getting professional treatment, aren't I?" She trembles like a leaf on the last branch of a tree. "I know how to ride the wave to wait out a feeling. I have tons of scented candles to sniff to calm me down. I soak in the tub and meditate and exercise every day. I come here and talk once a week. What else do I need to do?"

A hush falls throughout the room.

Thirty, sixty, then ninety days pass without our daughter dragging a razor across her skin.

By summer, she graduates from the outpatient treatment program.

Now when she rolls up her sleeves or drops her pants, the tiny red lines have faded to pale silver zigzags—tell tale reminders of her unhappiness about our divorce.

∼

THE LAST CARD IN THE DINETTE READING IS THE outcome, the answer to the question, "Can We Stop This

Divorce?" The card I draw is Judgment, a Major Arcana card, often associated with court proceedings or spiritual awakenings. A woman dressed as a slab of meat stands on a scale examining her weight. In the pale yellow background are advertisements for weight loss and diets. The woman bent over the scale wonders, Am I too fat? How much weight have I lost? Does the world only see me as I see myself—a slab of meat marked into sections for the butcher to slice? *The scale reads zero. A balance has been struck. A decision has been made. A judgment has been served. In our situation, I believe this card predicts the court finalizing our divorce.*

∼

DURING THE FIRST WEEK OF SUMMER, YOU AND I make our final trip to the mediator. We sit on opposite sides of the table, reviewing the final documents, which our attorneys have already signed and notarized.

The mediator asks for our licenses and writes our information in her notary journal.

I fiddle with the straps of my purse.

You slip on your reading glasses and sign your name first.

Afterward, I scrawl my signature and press my thumbprint in the notary journal.

Now the mediator will submit these final documents to the family court for the judge to review. As soon as he signs off, the documents will be recorded and a copy will be sent to each of us for our records.

The formality of this final gesture ending the

twenty-six years we've been together, almost twenty-four of them married, is bittersweet.

We step out into the warm summer sunshine. I squint and slip on my pair of prescription sunglasses. You offer to take me out to lunch before I head back to work and you head back to your computer repair shop.

"Sure," I say.

In a Mexican diner that was once a drive-in, we sit in a vinyl booth near the back and eat enchiladas and drink iced tea.

"Have you been here before?" I ask.

You nod, munching on a chip dipped in salsa. "My girlfriend and I come here on the weekends you stay at my house with the kids."

Your girlfriend. The phrase sounds odd although it shouldn't. We haven't been a couple in over a year.

After we push aside our plates and ask for doggie bags, you fold your arms on the table and lean forward. "Are you happy?"

That question, that innocent question, which sparked this whole divorce, returns full circle. I was never unhappy, was I? I just always wanted more—more time, more money, more romance, and sometimes more men. I scrunch the paper napkin in my lap and shrug. "Getting there," I say. "How about you?"

You nod. "I'm happy." Another long stare. "I want you to be happy too."

I bow my head. I know you do. I just don't know what it will take to get me there.

TAROT READING 4

WHERE DO WE GO FROM HERE?

Three Card Tarot Reading

week after the divorce is final, the Knight of Cups and I take four out of our five children to Kauai for our first family vacation. One afternoon, we lie on the beach and watch as a newlywed couple dressed in a tuxedo and a wedding gown pose for photographs. The Knight of Cups nudges my shoulder. "What advice would you give them?" He winks, thinking he is being funny. After all, we are Kurt

Russell and Goldie Hawn, two committed individuals whose relationship is cemented by mutual love and respect rather than the unrealistic expectations of marriage. But, staring at the newlyweds with their hopeful smiles, I feel a pang of loss and an undercurrent of desire. Tear prick my eyes. I scramble to my feet and cower behind the tailgate of the rental car beneath the shady palm trees and cry.

His son touches my shoulder. "What's wrong?"

His concern reaches through me. I open my mouth and hear the Knight of Cups' voice. "She's upset about that married couple. She wants to tell them they've wasted thousands of dollars on a wedding that will only end in thousands of dollars on a divorce."

"That's not what I'm upset about." I am angry he has broken his promises—to change the beneficiary of his life insurance policy from his ex-wife to me and to buy a house together with the proceeds from my divorce and the sale of his house.

We are not Goldie Hawn and Kurt Russell for there are no children to bind us, no real estate to unite us, and no comingling of two lives into a single one.

"Marry me, or I will move on," I tell him.

He says he'll have to think about it.

As soon as we return from vacation, I make an appointment to speak with Melanie. In a simple tarot reading, she draws two cards—the Devil and the King of Cups. Her interpretation is straightforward. "He's torn between being selfish and being generous of heart."

I sit beside her and nod. He wants the freedom of being single with the emotional support of marriage. "Which one will he choose?"

She slides the deck across the table and taps the top card.

I turn over the Ten of Cups, which depicts a family standing beneath a rainbow full of golden chalices—the happily-ever-after card in the tarot. I take a deep breath and release it slowly. I do not understand how the current tension between us will ever relax into this beautiful, blended family.

≈

IN APRIL 2018, THE KNIGHT OF CUPS AND I embark on a cruise ship bound for the western Caribbean. The humidity is low this early in the morning, but already I can feel the ends of my hair frizz and my skin stick with a thin layer of sweat.

Almost a year ago, he and I were in Kauai, wandering the trails leading to the Fern Grotto where lovers used to marry for a lifetime of good luck and happiness before the grottos became unsafe for tourists to enter. I stood on the platform overlooking the vacant mouths of the caves. He asked a couple to take our picture. I scooted close. He turned and fell to one knee. Holding up a diamond solitaire in a channel setting, he asked, "Will you marry me?"

The couple videotaped the proposal. Sometimes I ask him to replay the memory. On the tiny screen, I watch him fumble in his cargo shorts for the jewelry box. I inch closer. He turns and drops to one knee, holding up the ring in the box. I gasp, "Yes!" Without waiting, I grab the ring, slide it over my finger, and dance with the glittering star pressed against my chest.

When I told you about the engagement, you

stormed at me. "You have everything!" But then you calmed down.

I don't have *everything*.

I don't have *you*.

On the day of my second wedding, the Knight of Cups and I stand before the ship's captain in the back of a vacant restaurant near the bow of the ship to exchange our vows. I am dressed in a gown I bought at Brides and Maids. I did not want to wear the wedding dress my mother made for my first wedding. I wanted something new, something store bought, something that reflected who I am today. Although I fell in love with a golden ball gown, I eventually settled for a white slip dress, long and light, which easily folded into a suitcase without taking up too much space, and a silver headband full of tiny rosebuds and fake diamonds instead of a traditional veil. I wear five inch heels that elevate my height to my soon-to-be husband's shoulder and dust my lips with ruby lipstick to match the bouquet of blood red roses in my hands. He wears a dark blue suit, light blue shirt, and burgundy tie with a red rose pinned to the lapel.

The ship rocks, and my whole body sways.

He hides a snicker behind a hand.

I widen my smile and broaden my stance to avoid toppling against him or the captain.

Two ship employees witness the event I often doubted would happen.

The captain reminds us to encourage and support each other, to share a sense of humor, and to always hold each other's hearts with as much tenderness as we hold each other's hands. Glancing at each of us, he asks, "Will you promise to forsake all others till the end of your days together?"

A light, tingling sensation ripples from my crown to my toes. The captain said *till the end of our days together* and *not until death do us part*, which is the traditional saying. I doubt my ability to be faithful and loving until one of us dies, but I am confident I can carry my half of the relationship until we decide we no longer want to be together. "I do." Tilting up my chin, I smile.

"I will," the Knight of Cups says, squeezing my fingers.

The captain asks us to exchange rings.

The Knight of Cups slides the engagement ring on my finger because I didn't want a separate wedding band.

I wiggle a sterling silver ring inlaid with golden brown koa wood over his knuckle, which I purchased in Kauai. On the inside of the band, an image of the Hawaii Islands is engraved.

"I now pronounce you husband and wife." The captain says we may seal our promises with a kiss.

The Knight of Cups bends toward me, and I reach up toward him.

The brush of our lips is soft and fluttery like the hope in my heart.

～

LATER THAT SUMMER, YOU ANNOUNCE YOUR INTENTION to hold a commitment ceremony in Las Vegas. Neither you nor your girlfriend can ever marry if you both wish to continue to receive spousal support. The arrangement, which harkens to the days when gays and lesbians could not legally marry, is announced to relatives and friends.

I don't bother asking about your relationship with a tarot reading. I already know the card I would receive— the Lovers, a Major Arcana card of fate and destiny, the card of complimentary forces coming together, a commitment between soul mates or kindred spirits, or Plato's mythological reunion of two halves from one whole.

∼

I CANNOT ATTEND YOUR COMMITMENT CEREMONY. I must stay behind, caring for our son.

But I hear about the event through your sister who even shares some photographs with me.

You both arrive at the chapel early. You don't dress up in traditional wedding attire. You wear a black and white pin-striped zoot suit and your girlfriend wears a 1950's dress, platform sandals, and a pillbox hat with a tiny veil.

The heat in Las Vegas during the summer is criminal, pushing into the low hundreds. The suit and dress don't breathe, and the chapel is tiny and the air conditioner spotty. The vows are lighthearted, spoken before an Elvis impersonator, but the intent behind the words is serious and heartfelt. The commitment is real.

This is, after all, the woman you loved before you loved me.

Staring at the photographs, I can't help but remember our wedding, how young and hopeful and naïve we were—you standing outside the brick church with the best man, me walking down the aisle with my father—the reading from Corinthians about love being patient and kind, the exchange of vows and rings and the sealing kiss.

I smile at your smile and tell your sister you look happy.

I will not begrudge you for your happiness.

I will only mourn for the happiness we never had together.

∼

Even though we are with other people, I feel stuck, mired in that time of darkness and hatred, lies and deception, that ended with our divorce.

I consult with the tarot, as usual, and ask if we will ever heal. You seem, on the surface, to be content in your new life. I, on the other hand, twitch with rest-lessness.

The card I draw is yet another Major Arcana card —the Star.

As a child, I was told if I wished upon a star that wish would come true. Sometimes that happened. Other times it did not.

I hesitate to be infused with the hope promised by this card, which typically signifies optimism and peace.

After all, I cannot see a beacon in the darkness I am mired in. I cannot glimpse any stars in the night sky of my life. I can only focus on the inky black nothingness that surrounds me.

∼

During the three years since our divorce, we have stayed in touch beyond the requisite communication about our children or the financial support I am obligated to provide. Sometimes we send each other text messages or emails or chat on the phone like old friends. A few times we have met in vacant parking lots, back alleys, or behind the crumbling building where I work to exchange birthday or Christmas gifts and a token hug.

Today you have come by my new office to share lunch. Instead of being located in a condemned warehouse in Railroad Square beside the train tracks and a community park, the corporate headquarters has relocated to an oasis of dirt trails, a manmade pond, bridges, and a flagstone patio complete with picnic tables and barbecue pits. We carry the curry and rice dish I made last night and heated in the company's microwave just minutes ago over the bridge to the picnic tables on the flagstone patio. The dappled sunlight streams through whatever golden brown leaves remain on the overhead branches. The heat isn't as over-bearing as summer, but the threat of wildfires won't extinguish until the rains return later this fall.

You are dressed in a bright blue polo shirt and denim jeans and work shoes. I am dressed in my corporate attire—a standard dress and black flats. I don't wear heels anymore.

We are not here to discuss our twenty-four-year-old Forever Child who attends adult day care or our nineteen-year-old Princess Pea who just earned her real estate license. We are not here to discuss The Knight of Cups who recently retired or the Empress who recently became a first time grandma. We are not here to discuss your computer repair business or my job selling courses in forest therapy guide training or the new romance novel I've just sold to a small press. We are here to discuss our relationship, whatever there is left between us.

"I miss home cooked meals," you say, digging into the curry and rice. "We eat out too much."

I shrug and run the tines of my fork through the rice. "You never liked how I cooked."

You snicker. "*I* did most of the cooking."

I flash a crooked smile. "I know."

The breeze kicks up and blows the napkin off my lap. I trail after the flimsy paper as it tumbles like a leaf toward the pond. I snatch it up just in time. When I spin back toward the picnic tables, I catch you staring at me.

"You're still beautiful," you say, smiling.

"Thank you. You're still good looking yourself." And you are—broad and strong.

You shake your head. "I'm overweight. I never get to run anymore."

I sit and bow my head, remembering how you taught me how to run. That activity is now an integral part of my life, and I can't imagine starting my day without it. "Maybe I can watch our son, and you both can go to the track and run laps like we used to do."

You purse your lips and glance away. "She doesn't like running."

"What does she like to do?"

"Not much in terms of exercise."

My heart clenches in my chest. You love running as much as I love writing. "Teach her like you taught me."

"It's hard to retrain others at this late date." You finish the curry and rice and scoop out another serving. "We're not in our twenties. We're almost fifty."

I take a sip of water and stare at the sunlight dancing on the water. A family of ducks waddles across the grass in single file, from tallest to shortest. "I've been thinking of our relationship. I'm sorry I was never faithful. Please forgive me for breaking us."

"I've already forgiven you." You smile. "I hope you can learn to forgive yourself."

I shake my head as if that motion alone can clear the guilt and pain that continue to cloud my thoughts. "I want to get rid of so much in my life that doesn't serve me anymore."

"Sounds good." You reach across the table and offer your hand. "Just don't get rid of me. I like having you in my life. Even if we're no longer a couple."

I take your warm hand in my cool fingers and blink back the emotion welling in my eyes.

When the hour lunch is over, you walk me back to the office and help me wash and dry the dishes.

My boss strolls by and pauses to watch us for a moment, a smile playing at the edges of her lips.

I walk you to your car in the parking lot, and we embrace.

By the time I return to my desk, I feel so depleted I just want to go home and curl up in bed and make the world go away. I am overwhelmed by an unexpected rush of regret. I want to erase the last decade of my life. I want to start over…with you.

But that possibility does not exist.

How does one release the baggage of one's life and move onward?

I pull out my notebook and clock in to work. While I listen to voicemail, I think about our lives together. We had a good marriage once. Although a few years have passed since our divorce, we are still connected to each other. After all, we share children and a history, nothing can change that.

But there is something more, something I can't name that is growing between us.

My boss returns and sits at her desk across the room. "It's nice that you and your ex are friends."

I hang up the phone and glance in her direction, startled by the observation. I have never thought of you as my friend. But I guess, after everything we've gone through, it is the best relationship we can hope to have. "I left him, but I still love him." I tell her the truth, the truth I could never speak aloud because I was afraid the brittleness of the words would break me.

She nods. "Love never dies. It just changes or transforms." She gestures with her hands, forming an invisible ball of energy that twists and turns.

I nod, thankful for the imagery and the acknowledgment.

You are still my Magician—working your magic.

And I am forever your Fool—as eager to take a leap of faith as I am to make a mistake.

～

NOTES AND BIBLIOGRAPHY

Cynova, Melissa. *Tarot Elements: Five Readings to Reset Your Life*. Woodbury: Llewellyn Publications, 2019.

Fine, Sinead. Interview by Angela Lam. Facebook. Santa Rosa, California and Lotan, southern Israel, November 1-2, 2021.

Graham, Sasha. *Llewellyn's Complete Book of the Rider-Waite-Smith Tarot*. Woodbury: Llewellyn Publications, 2018.

Lape, Louise. Interview by Angela Lam. Zoom. Santa Rosa, California and Grofit, Israel, November 15, 2021.

Leszkiewicz, Anna, "Your Very Own Sylvia Plath," *New Statesman, UK Edition*, October 26, 2021.

Pollack, Rachel. Interview by Angela Lam. Zoom. Santa Rosa, California and New York, New York, October 28, 2021.

Quinn, Paul. *Tarot for Life: Reading the Cards for Everyday Guidance and Growth*. Wheaton: Quest Books, 2009.

Widso, Lynda. Interview by Angela Lam. Zoom. Santa Rosa, California and Pine Plains, New York, November 2, 2021.

Wisdo, Lynda. *Menopause in Crisis: When Spiritual Emergency Meets the Feminine Midlife Passage*. Scottsdale: Book Patch, 2015.

ACKNOWLEDGMENTS

First, thanks to God for asking me to write this story. For several years, I stalled, unable to put into words what I had experienced.

Thanks to Gotham Writers' Conference for the opportunity to meet with literary agents knowledgeable about the market and the direction this project needed to take.

Thanks to Nicole Zimmerman, fellow writer and instructor, accountability partner and friend. Our monthly meetings fueled this crazy journey.

Thanks to Kevin Gross for emotional and financial support. That inside joke we've shared for years—*You're my Theo and I'm your Van Gogh*—has brought levity and light to years of darkness.

Finally, and most importantly, thanks to Ed Turpin for over thirty years of love, friendship, inspiration, and support. You're still my Magician, and I'll forever be your Fool.